D1558436

FRANCISCO FRANCO

FRANCISCO FRANCO

Hedda Garza

CHELSEA HOUSE PUBLISHERS
NEW YORK
NEW HAVEN   PHILADELPHIA

EDITORIAL DIRECTOR: Nancy Toff
MANAGING EDITOR: Karyn Gullen Browne
COPY CHIEF: Perry Scott King
ART DIRECTOR: Giannella Garrett
PICTURE EDITOR: Elizabeth Terhune

Staff for FRANCISCO FRANCO:

SENIOR EDITOR: John W. Selfridge
ASSISTANT EDITORS: Maria Behan, Pierre Hauser, Kathleen McDermott, Bert Yaeger
COPY EDITORS: Gillian Bucky, Sean Dolan
DESIGN ASSISTANT: Jill Goldreyer
PICTURE RESEARCH: Juliette Dickstein
LAYOUT: David Murray
PRODUCTION COORDINATOR: Alma Rodriguez
PRODUCTION ASSISTANT: Karen Dreste
COVER ILLUSTRATION: Robin Peterson

CREATIVE DIRECTOR: Harold Steinberg

Franco Reprint

Frontispiece courtesy of AP/Wide World Photos

3 5 7 9 8 6 4 2
Library of Congress Cataloging in Publication Data

Garza, Hedda. FRANCISCO FRANCO

(World leaders past & present)
Bibliography: p.
Includes index.
1. Franco, Francisco, 1892–1975— Juvenile literature.
2. Spain—History—20th century— Juvenile literature.
3. Heads of state—Spain—Biography— Juvenile literature.
[1. Franco, Francisco, 1892–1975. 2. Spain—History—20th
century. 3. Heads of state] I. Title. II. Series.
DP264.F7G38   1987   946.082′092′4 [B] [92]   86-29963

ISBN 0-87754-524-3

Contents

JOHN ADAMS
JOHN QUINCY ADAMS
KONRAD ADENAUER
ALEXANDER THE GREAT
SALVADOR ALLENDE
MARC ANTONY
CORAZON AQUINO
YASIR ARAFAT
KING ARTHUR
HAFEZ AL-ASSAD
KEMAL ATATÜRK
ATTILA
CLEMENT ATTLEE
AUGUSTUS CAESAR
MENACHEM BEGIN
DAVID BEN-GURION
OTTO VON BISMARCK
LÉON BLUM
SIMON BOLÍVAR
CESARE BORGIA
WILLY BRANDT
LEONID BREZHNEV
JULIUS CAESAR
JOHN CALVIN
JIMMY CARTER
FIDEL CASTRO
CATHERINE THE GREAT
CHARLEMAGNE
CHIANG KAI-SHEK
WINSTON CHURCHILL
GEORGES CLEMENCEAU
CLEOPATRA
CONSTANTINE THE GREAT
HERNÁN CORTÉS
OLIVER CROMWELL
GEORGES-JACQUES
  DANTON
JEFFERSON DAVIS
MOSHE DAYAN
CHARLES DE GAULLE
EAMON DE VALERA
EUGENE DEBS
DENG XIAOPING
BENJAMIN DISRAELI
ALEXANDER DUBČEK
FRANÇOIS & JEAN-CLAUDE
  DUVALIER
DWIGHT EISENHOWER
ELEANOR OF AQUITAINE
ELIZABETH I
FAISAL
FERDINAND & ISABELLA
FRANCISCO FRANCO
BENJAMIN FRANKLIN

FREDERICK THE GREAT
INDIRA GANDHI
MOHANDAS GANDHI
GIUSEPPE GARIBALDI
AMIN & BASHIR GEMAYEL
GENGHIS KHAN
WILLIAM GLADSTONE
MIKHAIL GORBACHEV
ULYSSES S. GRANT
ERNESTO "CHE" GUEVARA
TENZIN GYATSO
ALEXANDER HAMILTON
DAG HAMMARSKJÖLD
HENRY VIII
HENRY OF NAVARRE
PAUL VON HINDENBURG
HIROHITO
ADOLF HITLER
HO CHI MINH
KING HUSSEIN
IVAN THE TERRIBLE
ANDREW JACKSON
JAMES I
WOJCIECH JARUZELSKI
THOMAS JEFFERSON
JOAN OF ARC
POPE JOHN XXIII
POPE JOHN PAUL II
LYNDON JOHNSON
BENITO JUÁREZ
JOHN KENNEDY
ROBERT KENNEDY
JOMO KENYATTA
AYATOLLAH KHOMEINI
NIKITA KHRUSHCHEV
KIM IL SUNG
MARTIN LUTHER KING, JR.
HENRY KISSINGER
KUBLAI KHAN
LAFAYETTE
ROBERT E. LEE
VLADIMIR LENIN
ABRAHAM LINCOLN
DAVID LLOYD GEORGE
LOUIS XIV
MARTIN LUTHER
JUDAS MACCABEUS
JAMES MADISON
NELSON & WINNIE
  MANDELA
MAO ZEDONG
FERDINAND MARCOS
GEORGE MARSHALL

MARY, QUEEN OF SCOTS
TOMÁŠ MASARYK
GOLDA MEIR
KLEMENS VON METTERNICH
JAMES MONROE
HOSNI MUBARAK
ROBERT MUGABE
BENITO MUSSOLINI
NAPOLÉON BONAPARTE
GAMAL ABDEL NASSER
JAWAHARLAL NEHRU
NERO
NICHOLAS II
RICHARD NIXON
KWAME NKRUMAH
DANIEL ORTEGA
MOHAMMED REZA PAHLAVI
THOMAS PAINE
CHARLES STEWART
  PARNELL
PERICLES
JUAN PERÓN
PETER THE GREAT
POL POT
MUAMMAR EL-QADDAFI
RONALD REAGAN
CARDINAL RICHELIEU
MAXIMILIEN ROBESPIERRE
ELEANOR ROOSEVELT
FRANKLIN ROOSEVELT
THEODORE ROOSEVELT
ANWAR SADAT
HAILE SELASSIE
PRINCE SIHANOUK
JAN SMUTS
JOSEPH STALIN
SUKARNO
SUN YAT-SEN
TAMERLANE
MOTHER TERESA
MARGARET THATCHER
JOSIP BROZ TITO
TOUSSAINT L'OUVERTURE
LEON TROTSKY
PIERRE TRUDEAU
HARRY TRUMAN
QUEEN VICTORIA
LECH WALESA
GEORGE WASHINGTON
CHAIM WEIZMANN
WOODROW WILSON
XERXES
EMILIANO ZAPATA
ZHOU ENLAI

CHELSEA HOUSE PUBLISHERS

ON LEADERSHIP

Arthur M. Schlesinger, jr.

LEADERSHIP, it may be said, is really what makes the world go round. Love no doubt smooths the passage; but love is a private transaction between consenting adults. Leadership is a public transaction with history. The idea of leadership affirms the capacity of individuals to move, inspire, and mobilize masses of people so that they act together in pursuit of an end. Sometimes leadership serves good purposes, sometimes bad; but whether the end is benign or evil, great leaders are those men and women who leave their personal stamp on history.

Now, the very concept of leadership implies the proposition that individuals can make a difference. This proposition has never been universally accepted. From classical times to the present day, eminent thinkers have regarded individuals as no more than the agents and pawns of larger forces, whether the gods and goddesses of the ancient world or, in the modern era, race, class, nation, the dialectic, the will of the people, the spirit of the times, history itself. Against such forces, the individual dwindles into insignificance.

So contends the thesis of historical determinism. Tolstoy's great novel *War and Peace* offers a famous statement of the case. Why, Tolstoy asked, did millions of men in the Napoleonic Wars, denying their human feelings and their common sense, move back and forth across Europe slaughtering their fellows? "The war," Tolstoy answered, "was bound to happen simply because it was bound to happen." All prior history predetermined it. As for leaders, they, Tolstoy said, "are but the labels that serve to give a name to an end and, like labels, they have the least possible connection with the event." The greater the leader, "the more conspicuous the inevitability and the predestination of every act he commits." The leader, said Tolstoy, is "the slave of history."

Determinism takes many forms. Marxism is the determinism of class. Nazism the determinism of race. But the idea of men and women as the slaves of history runs athwart the deepest human instincts. Rigid determinism abolishes the idea of human freedom—

the assumption of free choice that underlies every move we make, every word we speak, every thought we think. It abolishes the idea of human responsibility, since it is manifestly unfair to reward or punish people for actions that are by definition beyond their control. No one can live consistently by any deterministic creed. The Marxist states prove this themselves by their extreme susceptibility to the cult of leadership.

More than that, history refutes the idea that individuals make no difference. In December 1931 a British politician crossing Park Avenue in New York City between 76th and 77th Streets around 10:30 P.M. looked in the wrong direction and was knocked down by an automobile—a moment, he later recalled, of a man aghast, a world aglare: "I do not understand why I was not broken like an eggshell or squashed like a gooseberry." Fourteen months later an American politician, sitting in an open car in Miami, Florida, was fired on by an assassin; the man beside him was hit. Those who believe that individuals make no difference to history might well ponder whether the next two decades would have been the same had Mario Constasino's car killed Winston Churchill in 1931 and Giuseppe Zangara's bullet killed Franklin Roosevelt in 1933. Suppose, in addition, that Adolf Hitler had been killed in the street fighting during the Munich *Putsch* of 1923 and that Lenin had died of typhus during World War I. What would the 20th century be like now?

For better or for worse, individuals do make a difference. "The notion that a people can run itself and its affairs anonymously," wrote the philosopher William James, "is now well known to be the silliest of absurdities. Mankind does nothing save through initiatives on the part of inventors, great or small, and imitation by the rest of us—these are the sole factors in human progress. Individuals of genius show the way, and set the patterns, which common people then adopt and follow."

Leadership, James suggests, means leadership in thought as well as in action. In the long run, leaders in thought may well make the greater difference to the world. But, as Woodrow Wilson once said, "Those only are leaders of men, in the general eye, who lead in action. . . . It is at their hands that new thought gets its translation into the crude language of deeds." Leaders in thought often invent in solitude and obscurity, leaving to later generations the tasks of imitation. Leaders in action—the leaders portrayed in this series—have to be effective in their own time.

And they cannot be effective by themselves. They must act in response to the rhythms of their age. Their genius must be adapted, in a phrase of William James's, "to the receptivities of the moment." Leaders are useless without followers. "There goes the mob," said the French politician hearing a clamor in the streets. "I am their leader. I must follow them." Great leaders turn the inchoate emotions of the mob to purposes of their own. They seize on the opportunities of their time, the hopes, fears, frustrations, crises, potentialities. They succeed when events have prepared the way for them, when the community is awaiting to be aroused, when they can provide the clarifying and organizing ideas. Leadership ignites the circuit between the individual and the mass and thereby alters history.

It may alter history for better or for worse. Leaders have been responsible for the most extravagant follies and most monstrous crimes that have beset suffering humanity. They have also been vital in such gains as humanity has made in individual freedom, religious and racial tolerance, social justice, and respect for human rights.

There is no sure way to tell in advance who is going to lead for good and who for evil. But a glance at the gallery of men and women in *World Leaders—Past and Present* suggests some useful tests.

One test is this: Do leaders lead by force or by persuasion? By command or by consent? Through most of history leadership was exercised by the divine right of authority. The duty of followers was to defer and to obey. "Theirs not to reason why / Theirs but to do and die." On occasion, as with the so-called enlightened despots of the 18th century in Europe, absolutist leadership was animated by humane purposes. More often, absolutism nourished the passion for domination, land, gold, and conquest and resulted in tyranny.

The great revolution of modern times has been the revolution of equality. The idea that all people should be equal in their legal condition has undermined the old structure of authority, hierarchy, and deference. The revolution of equality has had two contrary effects on the nature of leadership. For equality, as Alexis de Tocqueville pointed out in his great study *Democracy in America*, might mean equality in servitude as well as equality in freedom.

"I know of only two methods of establishing equality in the political world," Tocqueville wrote. "Rights must be given to every citizen, or none at all to anyone . . . save one, who is the master of all." There was no middle ground "between the sovereignty of all and the absolute power of one man." In his astonishing prediction of 20th-century totalitarian dictatorship, Tocqueville explained how the revolution of equality could lead to the *"Führerprinzip"* and more terrible absolutism than the world had ever known.

But when rights are given to every citizen and the sovereignty of all is established, the problem of leadership takes a new form, becomes more exacting than ever before. It is easy to issue commands and enforce them by the rope and the stake, the concentration camp and the *gulag.* It is much harder to use argument and achievement to overcome opposition and win consent. The Founding Fathers of the United States understood the difficulty. They believed that history had given them the opportunity to decide, as Alexander Hamilton wrote in the first Federalist Paper, whether men are indeed capable of basing government on "reflection and choice, or whether they are forever destined to depend . . . on accident and force."

Government by reflection and choice called for a new style of leadership and a new quality of followership. It required leaders to be responsive to popular concerns, and it required followers to be active and informed participants in the process. Democracy does not eliminate emotion from politics; sometimes it fosters demagoguery; but it is confident that, as the greatest of democratic leaders put it, you cannot fool all of the people all of the time. It measures leadership by results and retires those who overreach or falter or fail.

It is true that in the long run despots are measured by results too. But they can postpone the day of judgment, sometimes indefinitely, and in the meantime they can do infinite harm. It is also true that democracy is no guarantee of virtue and intelligence in government, for the voice of the people is not necessarily the voice of God. But democracy, by assuring the right of opposition, offers built-in resistance to the evils inherent in absolutism. As the theologian Reinhold Niebuhr summed it up, "Man's capacity for justice makes democracy possible, but man's inclination to injustice makes democracy necessary."

A second test for leadership is the end for which power is sought. When leaders have as their goal the supremacy of a master race or the promotion of totalitarian revolution or the acquisition and exploitation of colonies or the protection of greed and privilege or the preservation of personal power, it is likely that their leadership will do little to advance the cause of humanity. When their goal is the abolition of slavery, the liberation of women, the enlargement of opportunity for the poor and powerless, the extension of equal rights to racial minorities, the defense of the freedoms of expression and opposition, it is likely that their leadership will increase the sum of human liberty and welfare.

Leaders have done great harm to the world. They have also conferred great benefits. You will find both sorts in this series. Even "good" leaders must be regarded with a certain wariness. Leaders are not demigods; they put on their trousers one leg after another just like ordinary mortals. No leader is infallible, and every leader needs to be reminded of this at regular intervals. Irreverence irritates leaders but is their salvation. Unquestioning submission corrupts leaders and demeans followers. Making a cult of a leader is always a mistake. Fortunately hero worship generates its own antidote. "Every hero," said Emerson, "becomes a bore at last."

The signal benefit the great leaders confer is to embolden the rest of us to live according to our own best selves, to be active, insistent, and resolute in affirming our own sense of things. For great leaders attest to the reality of human freedom against the supposed inevitabilities of history. And they attest to the wisdom and power that may lie within the most unlikely of us, which is why Abraham Lincoln remains the supreme example of great leadership. A great leader, said Emerson, exhibits new possibilities to all humanity. "We feed on genius. . . . Great men exist that there may be greater men."

Great leaders, in short, justify themselves by emancipating and empowering their followers. So humanity struggles to master its destiny, remembering with Alexis de Tocqueville: "It is true that around every man a fatal circle is traced beyond which he cannot pass; but within the wide verge of that circle he is powerful and free; as it is with man, so with communities."

1

A Bad Time to Be Born

In 1936 the menace of Adolf Hitler's Nazi Germany was hanging over the world. Members of unions, Jews, anti-Nazis of every description, were trying to escape torture and death in concentration camps. Hitler had gone public with his plans. "Today we rule Germany, tomorrow the world," he had roared to cheering throngs.

Hitler had already enlisted Italy's fascist dictator, Benito Mussolini, in his schemes for empire. The two leaders were sending sophisticated war machinery and soldiers into Spain to help the insurgent Nationalist general, Francisco Franco, topple the Spanish Republic, a fragile democracy. The Western democracies had refused to come to the aid of the beleaguered republic. Some American businessmen were making fortunes selling oil and arms to Germany and Italy.

As they listened to the news on their radios, many Americans discussed the sham of American "neutrality," believing that their government, along with the governments of France and Great Britain, were making a terrible mistake by not curtailing the rise of fascism in Europe. They agreed that if Spain was lost to the fascists, Hitler and Mussolini would go on to overrun the world. Some of the Americans decided to back their beliefs with action; they would volunteer to fight, to die if necessary, to stop the rise of fascism in Spain.

Our regime is based on bayonets and blood, not on hypocritical elections.
—FRANCISCO FRANCO

General Francisco Franco, leader of the Nationalist uprising during the Spanish Civil War (1936–39). Taking advantage of Spain's political instability, Franco toppled the reigning democratic government and established a fascist state that remained in power for over 40 years.

Fascist Italy's Benito Mussolini and Nazi Germany's Adolf Hitler stand at attention for this 1936 portrait. Sensing kinship with the policies of Franco, these powerful dictators lent aid and support to the Spanish general during the civil war.

SNARK/ART RESOURCE

The dead were piled in the street, almost a story high, and burnt. The engineers kept pouring gasoline until the remains sank down. . . . The whole town stank of burning flesh.

—BILL BAILEY
U.S. volunteer in the
International Brigades, on
the fighting in
northern Spain

In December of that year young men from all over America came to New York to enlist in the cause of freedom. Some came on buses; some thumbed rides. Among them were factory workers, longshoremen, students, and labor-union organizers. They were Catholics, Protestants, Jews, and atheists; they were black and white. But they all had the same reason for assembling in New York.

On December 26, they crowded into the third-class quarters of the French luxury liner S.S. *Normandie*. Their passports were stamped "Not for Travel to Spain." It was the first time the government had officially restricted travel. Americans could still travel to Nazi Germany or fascist Italy — but not to Spain. Two days before their ship arrived at Le Havre, France, a news bulletin came on the radio. "Chairman McReynolds of the House Foreign Affairs Committee declared he would urge the De-

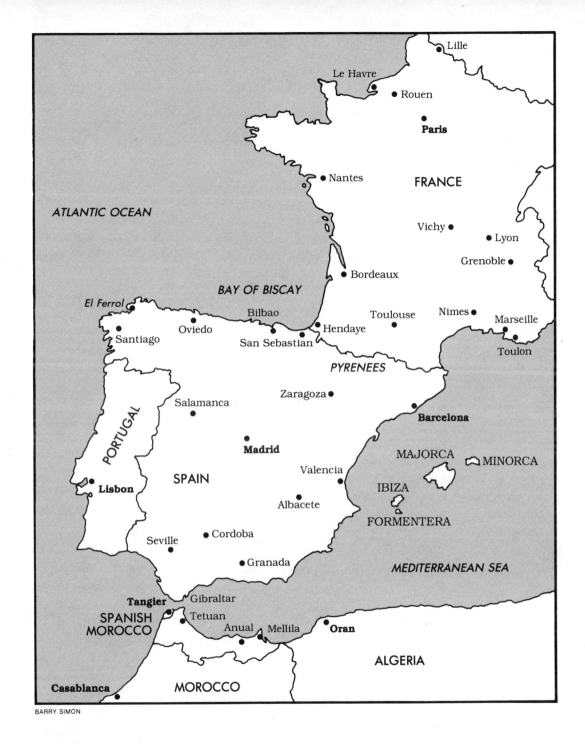

BARRY SIMON

As Franco's troops raged through Spain, the antifascist
International Brigades, made up of volunteers from
throughout the world, poured in from France over the
Pyrenees to support the faltering Spanish Republic.

15

partment of Justice to apply the section of the criminal code providing a $3,000 fine or a year in prison for enlistment of Americans in a foreign war."

When the boat docked, not one man turned back. All 95 crossed the icy, snowcapped Pyrenees mountains between France and Spain, slipped across the border and finally arrived at Albacete, Spain, on January 6, 1937. In the next few months over 3,000 more American men and women would follow.

They would be part of the XV International Brigade — the Abraham Lincoln and George Washington Battalions. They would join 40,000 men and women from around the world — French and British volunteers, Italian antifascists, German anti-Nazis, Canadians, Russians, Hungarians, and others —

This poster for a record — "Sons of the Town, Man the Barricades" — is dedicated to "the victims of fascism." Posters of this type were common during the Spanish Civil War, demonstrating the popular appeal of the anti-fascist movement.

16

Enlistees of the Republican forces. During the revolution Franco's Nationalist forces did not fight a well-trained army of disciplined soldiers, but rather common men, women, and children.

united against oppression. The first 500 European volunteers had arrived in Spain two months before and had already fought a victorious battle to save Madrid, the capital of Spain, from the talons of fascism.

The International Brigades were viewed by many as crusaders. They went to Spain, often against their own countries' policies, not for money or for fame but because they believed in democracy. Half of them would die for this belief, their bodies remaining on the Spanish soil where they fell.

Veterans of the Abraham Lincoln Battalion who would be fortunate enough to return home two years later would meet an unfriendly reception. Efforts would be made to smear their names, and some would be prevented from fighting overseas during World War II. Still, 900 of them would see active duty

THE BETTMANN ARCHIVE

Fighting from trucks, walls, trenches, and rooftops, Spanish loyalists make a valiant attempt to prevent the fall of the capital city of Madrid. Aided by the International Brigades, these passionate republicans managed to repel the fascists for almost three years.

and 400 would die in Europe and the South Pacific. During the 1950s Cold War period, they would be blacklisted from jobs as "reds" and "traitors." In 1955 the Subversive Activities Control Board would rule that their organization, the Veterans of the Abraham Lincoln Brigade, had to register with the U.S. Justice Department as a communist front organization.

Despite the smear campaign, millions of Americans would come to know the truth — that the American volunteers had gone to Spain, poorly equipped and with neither training nor support, to fight fascism and defend democracy. They left their brothers and sisters in unmarked graves in towns like Teruel, Belchite, Brunete, Villanueva de la Cañada, or alongside the Ebro and Jarama rivers. They would learn that no group of Americans had ever made such conscientious and willing sacrifices in the name of liberty.

From February 1937 until September of 1938 — 20 months without leave or liberty — the volunteers fought side by side, bandaging one another's wounds and giving their blood to each other in makeshift hospitals in a life-or-death effort to stop Francisco Franco, the leader of the Spanish fascists, and to secure the Spanish Republic.

Years later, a member of the Abraham Lincoln Battalion said: "We fought for what we believed; perhaps, if the democracies had acted as we did, there would have been no second world war and the millions dead in that conflict might have lived to old age in peace and love, instead of war and hatred. I was convinced in '37 and am still convinced that the cause of the Spanish Republic was a just one. I would do it again even at the cost of my life. For me, the words of La Pasionaria will always hold true: 'It is better to die on your feet than to live on your knees.' "

Francisco Franco would rule Spain for almost 40 years, crushing it under an iron jackboot of censorship, torture, and death. But this powerful tyrant began his life as the undersized son of an obscure naval paymaster in a small port. He was expected to follow his father's footsteps into the administrative officer corps of the Spanish navy.

Franco's birthplace was El Ferrol, a village overlooking the Atlantic Ocean in the region of Galicia, in northwestern Spain. Born at 12:30 A.M. on December 4, 1892, he was christened with many names, customary in Spanish society — Francisco Paulino Hermenegildo Teódulo Franco y Bahamonde — the last name being his mother's family name, but for most of his life he was known simply as Franco.

At the time of Franco's birth the glory days of the Spanish conquest of the Americas and control of the high seas were long gone, but El Ferrol still sported the remnants of those times. During earlier centuries, as Spanish explorers subdued and enslaved the people of South America, the Caribbean,

Cuban patriot and poet José Martí led the Cuban revolution of 1895. Although unsuccessful, this rebellion demonstrated the weakness of the antiquated Spanish Empire.

northern Africa, and the far-flung Pacific territories of the Philippines and Guam, more harbors were needed in Spain to receive the ships carrying the loot taken from the colonies. In 1726 El Ferrol was made the headquarters of a naval command, and it quickly grew into a major port.

Franco's ancestors from the south of Spain came to El Ferrol during this period of growth. His father, Nicolás Franco y Salgado-Aranjo, became the fourth man in the family line to become a naval officer, receiving his commission in 1878. In the Spanish navy rapid promotion traditionally had been given to battle heroes, but Nicolás was too late for that. Fifty years earlier, a battle for liberation had swept the South American continent and Mexico, driving out the Spanish occupiers. Now Great Britain and the United States had won hegemony over South America and its resources, building their empires and their navies. There were no more brave expeditions into new territories; there was only a des-

The sinking of the U.S. *Merrimac* during the Spanish-American War in June 1898. Although the Spanish fought valiantly, the invading U.S. forces proved unstoppable, and Spain was forced to sign the humiliating Treaty of Paris on December 10, 1898.

perate effort to hold on to the few remnants of the Spanish empire, most importantly Cuba, Puerto Rico, Guam, the Philippines, and Spanish Morocco, in the deserts of northwestern Africa.

Nicolás Franco made a few routine trips to the Philippines, but during most of his career he served in naval offices, supervising payrolls and supply purchases. He compensated for the dullness of his job by drinking and chasing women. In 1890, at the age of 36, he married María del Pilar Bahamonde y Pardo de Andrade, the daughter of a senior officer in his department. From the point of view of status and titles, he had made a "good match." Pilar's father came from a landowning family, and her mother's family had been in El Ferrol for centuries.

The marriage, however, was doomed from the start. Pilar, a petite young woman with an oval face and sad, brown eyes, was a devout Catholic. Quiet, dignified, and serious, Pilar lived according to ideals of charity, morality, and duty. By contrast, her new husband cared little for religious affairs. Nicolás paraded through the town, handsome in his uniform, laughing, joking, drinking, and womanizing just as he had before his marriage. Pilar must have wept and prayed in private, but in public she displayed great calm and dignity, complaining to no one.

The newlyweds lived in a three-story balconied and terraced stone house at 136 Calle del Sol, right off El Ferrol's main plaza. A little more than a year after their marriage, a son, named Nicolás after his father, was born, and toward the end of the following year came Francisco. There were three more children—Pilar, Ramón, and Pazita.

Nicolás's work and private recreation meant that he was scarcely ever at home. Given a very modest allowance to cover expenses, Pilar managed to scrape by and keep up appearances. Of all the children, Francisco, called "Paquito" by his family, seemed most hurt by his father's absence and his mother's unhappiness. His older brother, Nicolás, and his younger brother, Ramón, were both like his father, extroverted and carefree. But Francisco drew more and more into a shell, becoming very shy and introverted.

Defeated by the superior forces of the United States during the Spanish-American War, the last remnant of the Spanish army stands at attention outside the governor's palace in Havana, Cuba.

Franco took after his mother in many respects. He was an undersized child who would grow to a full height of only five feet three inches; he had small hands and feet, soft hazel eyes, and a full mouth. Fishing and swimming with the other boys, kicking a soccer ball, and playing pirate, he daydreamed of a naval career, not behind a desk like his father, but as a warrior.

By the time of Francisco's sixth birthday, not only his future but the future of El Ferrol and all Spain looked bleak. Spain was losing most of its few remaining precious colonies. Guerrilla fighters on Cuba, originally led by poet José Martí, who died in battle in 1895, and then led by the Afro-Cuban hero Antonio Maceo, were smashing Spain's armed forces. Only 90 miles from Cuba, the United States was eyeing Spain's nearby Caribbean colonies. For a while, public opinion in the United States prevented the government from giving full-scale backing to the Cuban rebels. Many Americans believed that the wealthy entrepreneurs who professed an interest in Cuba were only motivated by the profits they might acquire and had no real concern for Cuban liberation. These Americans were unwilling to risk the lives of their sons to fill the pockets of the rich.

The corrupt Spanish government tried to stave off American intervention by offering a few concessions to the Cubans and special trade terms in Cuba to U.S. companies. But it was too late. On the night of February 15, 1898, the U.S. battleship *Maine*, berthed in Havana harbor, was rocked by a mysterious explosion and sank. Over 260 men were lost. U.S. public opinion changed overnight. With the increased demand for U.S. intervention, Congress declared Cuba independent and demanded Spain's withdrawal from the island. By the end of April 1898 the Spanish-American War was in full swing.

The results were predictable. The United States was wealthy, strong at sea, and fighting on its own doorstep. Spain was weak militarily and thousands of miles from Cuba. Years later Franco wrote, "The government rushed into the war without plans or resources and in a defeatist spirit; and, despite the

An 1894 French magazine cover depicts the execution of six anarchists in Barcelona, Spain. The generation raised after the Spanish-American War repudiated the old conventions of colonialism, militarism, and monarchy in favor of freedom of thought and representative government.

high morale of the fighting men, the plunder was consummated." There was one humiliating defeat after another for the Spanish navy, and on December 10, 1898, just after Franco's sixth birthday, Spain signed the Treaty of Paris. Under the treaty's terms Spain withdrew from Cuba and ceded Puerto Rico, Guam, and the Philippines to the United States.

These defeats, first by the Cubans, then by the Americans, were called *El desastre* ("the disaster"). The rebellious colony of Spanish Morocco, opposite Spain across the Straits of Gibraltar, in northwestern Africa, grew in importance to Spain. Those

Spaniards growing up in that period, young men and women with little hope for the future, were called "the generation of '98." The shock ran deep. Two battle fleets had been destroyed — and worse yet, by an upstart Protestant country with little culture or history. A sense of national humiliation pervaded the country.

As the crippled troopships limped into El Ferrol and other ports, broken, fever-ridden soldiers and sailors were brought from their decks. With fewer ships docking in the harbor, economic hardship fell on the town. There were no jobs for the dockworkers and the need for naval officers lessened. For Pilar Franco, it was just one more blow in a miserable life. Promotion was now out of the question for her husband. As to future plans for her sons, cadetships in the naval executive branch were restricted to 10 a year.

Miles away from El Ferrol, the spirit of popular rebellion filled the air. In the north, and especially in the region of Catalonia, wealthy industrialists had grown fat on the income received from the labors of the Cuban, Puerto Rican, and Philippine people, unconcerned that the local peasants and workers lived in abject poverty. In the south, 3 million landless peasants, always on the edge of starvation, roamed the countryside in search of work. Almost a quarter of a million ordinary Spaniards, mostly the sons of the poor, had died of wounds or yellow fever in Cuba and Puerto Rico for a cause of the wealthy that had brought them only defeat.

Intellectuals of the generation of 1898 urged a new era of education, development, and political democracy if Spain were to advance. They demanded land reform for the peasants and better pay for the workers. They launched an attack on the ruling classes of Spain, on the whole concept of colonialism and dominance, chipping away at the basic idea that the Spanish king, military, and the Catholic church had been placed in their position by the authority of God. Many workers joined the intellectuals in an upsurge of revulsion against the military. A new movement was born in the region of Catalonia, specifically in the province of Barcelona — the anarchist

We have need of history in its entirety, not to fall back into it, but to escape from it.
—JOSÉ ORTEGA Y GASSET
Spanish philosopher of
"the generation of '98"

UPI/BETTMANN NEWSPHOTOS

A view of the picturesque Basque region in northern Spain. The anarchist movement, bent on bringing a new political and social order to Spain, became especially popular among the fiercely independent people of this mountainous area.

movement, bent on destroying the old controlling forces in Spain. Anarchism was especially popular among the working classes.

As it had done in Cuba, the Spanish government used strong-arm tactics to suppress the criticisms. Hundreds of trade unionists were arrested, tortured, and executed. But the terror campaign only strengthened the people's resolve to change things.

Francisco Franco grew up insulated from the new democratic and anarchist ideas sweeping Spain. Almost everyone in El Ferrol supported the view of the aristocrats and military that "the disaster" had been caused by the liberals, by their numerous concessions in the guise of reforms.

Sent to a small, private Catholic school, the College of the Sacred Heart, Franco was taught to obey and not ask questions. Later, at the age of 12, he followed his brother Nicolás into the Naval Preparatory Academy, run by a naval officer who was obsessed with military history. Franco learned to admire Spanish warriors and conquerors. He drank in and forever believed the grandiose imperialist vision of Spain as a conveyor of Christianity and civilization to the Americas and other underdeveloped regions of the world. He came to hate those who advocated democracy. He was taught that Spain could advance only under strong leaders and would be destroyed if the lower classes had a voice. Law and order was the only flag of progress — the law and order of a strong state and a strong church. His password became "the stick—applied heavily."

His brother Nicolás won a place in the Naval Academy in 1905 when he was only 14, but just two years later admissions to the academy were suspended due to a national financial crisis. Franco's application was turned down. Since his only ambition was to join the military, Franco would have to take second best — the army. With the army concentrating on subduing internal protest and maintaining the colony of Spanish Morocco, the Infantry Academy at Toledo was admitting as many cadets as possible. On August 29, 1907, notified of his acceptance, Franco said good-bye to his beloved mother. Now 15 years old but still the size of a boy, Franco set out for Toledo to try to make the most of an army career.

His first months at the infantry college were miserable. He was not only the youngest and smallest of the new students, but he had a high, shrill voice. He became the victim of every practical joke in the barracks. His clothes and books were hidden, and objects were often hurled at him. He studied hard, though, and tried to keep out of the way of the bigger boys.

His education continued to be traditionalist, Catholic, and monarchist. Britain and France were enemies, trying to take away Spain's colonies in Africa. Germany was a great military power to be imitated and admired. The United States was an

King Alfonso XIII. Although rightful ruler of Spain Alfonso was little more than a figurehead, allowing the strongest party in government to make the critical decisions.

Moroccan tribesmen are honored by Spanish troops for
their assistance in fighting rebel tribes. In the early
1900s Spanish Morocco, a last remnant of Spain's empire, was a region of unending war — a veritable paradise
for Spanish soldiers, like Franco, seeking glory.

uncouth Protestant braggart, preaching democracy while gobbling up the former territories of Spanish America. Democracy was unsuited to Spain and would cause anarchy, socialism, or communism. The army must defend Spain against foreign and internal enemies.

This image of Spain was far different from that of the Spain of humanist and liberal education taught in other schools. The spirit of free inquiry was never encouraged at the military academy. Franco studied battle strategy and often sang the academy's anthem, directed to King Alfonso XIII: "You will still have your faithful infantry which knows how to vanquish for it knows how to die." He was to remain anchored for the rest of his life in the narrow nationalism of his childhood, without questioning duty, loyalty to those in power, and discipline, while harboring a deep prejudice against intellectuals and all those who worked for social reform.

The ideals of the military were not often the ideals of the people it controlled. In 1909, two years after Franco entered the Toledo academy, the native tribesmen of Morocco, called Moors by the Spaniards, rose up against their Spanish rulers. The war minister of Spain announced that he was ready to conscript young Spaniards into the army to put down the revolt. In Barcelona, workers rioted in protest against the decision. Police attacked the demonstrators; many were killed or jailed and tortured during the "Tragic Week," as it was called. Before it was over, 120 people were dead, and 60 government buildings and churches had been burned down by the angry protesters.

At the academy the war minister's proclamation was viewed in a more favorable light. Francisco and the other boys discussed the events over their meals and argued over the tactics for controlling the mobs in the cities and beating back the rebels in Morocco.

On July 13, 1910, at the age of 18, Francisco Franco graduated from the Infantry Academy with honors. In Morocco, rebellious tribesmen were successfully taking on the Spanish army, and Franco longed to fight his first battle.

2

A Soldier in Africa

When Franco's orders for his transfer to Morocco arrived in February 1912, the young officer was excited. It had been almost two years since he had graduated from the academy, and his sole tour of duty had been in the garrison of his home village of El Ferrol.

Arriving in Melilla, Spanish Morocco, on February 24, Franco immediately took his position as second lieutenant in the Spanish army's 68th Regiment. According to Brian Crozier, a biographer of Franco, one of the army's most vicious enemies was the Moroccan weather: "It was a violent climate, changing from heat to cold with dramatic suddenness. . . . Winter brought furious snowstorms, and summer, stupefying heat. When day changed to night, the thermometer would plummet twenty or thirty degrees. The men would emerge from their tents, ears and throats wrapped tight against the penetrating cold, only to tear off scarves and sweaters when the first heat of the sun attacked them." The sense of adventure that Franco had hoped to gain from fighting the Moorish guerrillas was, however, still missing.

In this land of life and mystery, we must not walk in darkness. We must lift the veil and identify ourselves with the Moroccan way of thinking.
—FRANCISCO FRANCO
on the Spanish military
presence in Morocco, 1924

Cadet Francisco Franco at the Toledo Infantry Academy. Military school helped Franco become a master of battle strategy and develop a sense of iron discipline. Two years later he would get a chance to apply his lessons in the deserts of Spanish Morocco as a second lieutenant in the Spanish army.

Franco's wife, Carmen Polo y Martínez Valdés. Though engaged in 1917, they would not wed for another six years because of his absences during his military career in Morocco.

Weeks after his arrival, when the second lieutenant heard of a "native police" force being organized by the prestigious Spanish General Dámaso Berenguer, he immediately volunteered for one of the force's command positions. The *Regulares Indígenas* (Regular Native Forces), as it came to be known later, was an organization manned by Moorish recruits and led by Spanish officers. Within the span of a year this corps became the vanguard of the Spanish army in Morocco. Franco would finally get to see some action.

On May 14, 1912, the Regulares were ordered to attack the rebel city of Hadda-Allal-u-Kaddar. Spanish scouts had sighted the great Moroccan rebel leader El Mizián there. Under heavy fire, the Regulares made their way to the city. During this onslaught two significant events occurred: El Mizián was killed by a Spanish sniper's bullet, thus effectively destroying Moroccan resistance in the area, and Franco was noticed by General Berenguer as a fine, upcoming military commander. Two months later Franco was promoted to first lieutenant.

By January 1915 Franco had made captain at the unprecedented age of 22. He had earned quite a reputation as a skilled commander and as a tough soldier. Then, in June 1916, he was seriously wounded by enemy gunfire. Undaunted, he returned to active duty soon after recovering from his wound, and he was shortly promoted to major.

Franco (bottom, center) and his commander, General José Millán Astray (bottom, third from right) pose with other members of the Spanish Foreign Legion. Following their motto — "Long Live Death!" — this corps of soldiers struck fear into the hearts of rebel Moroccans.

UPI/BETTMANN NEWSPHOTOS

General Miguel Primo de Rivera meets with a Moroccan prince in Madrid in 1924. In a move that outraged Franco, Primo de Rivera announced that Spanish Morocco would have to be sacrificed for the good of Spain.

Franco returned to Spain in March 1917, assuming a position in the Prince's Regiment stationed at Oviedo, the capital of the region of Asturias in northern Spain. The veteran of the conflict in Morocco quickly became a local celebrity, attracting the attention of admirers. Señorita Carmen Polo y Martínez Valdés, one of Franco's female fans, became his fiancée. Their marriage was deferred, however, for in 1920 Franco received another call to active duty.

In October Franco returned to Spanish Morocco to serve as second in command to General José Millán Astray of the newly formed Spanish Foreign Legion. Three thousand men from all over the world had been recruited by Millán Astray under the warrior's slogan of "Long Live Death!" They were an odd assortment of men with only one thing in common: for high pay they were willing to kill any assigned enemy. Franco found them very different from his former troops, the Regulares. The legionnaires were older men, many from violent backgrounds, paid killers whom Franco described as "shipwrecked from life." Among them were escaped criminals, exiles from Latin America, discharged World War I German soldiers who could not adjust to peacetime, a black boxer fleeing from racial prejudice in the United States, and even a former circus clown.

Franco quickly got down to the business of training these men. The bloodthirsty legionnaires became restless without real action and fought among themselves or engaged in the pastime of spotting enemies, murdering them, and mutilating their bodies in order to take body parts back to camp as physical proof of their prowess. Franco himself felt the need for more than brief forays against snipers and guerrilla bands to achieve further glory.

After a year of inactivity, a humiliating defeat for Spain gave Franco his chance. On July 21, 1921, at Annual, the forces of Moroccan independence leader Muhammad Abd el-Krim put to rout Spain's main army, led by General Manuel Fernández Silvestre. In three days, the Spanish army lost 16,000 men and the territorial gains of 12 years. The disgraced Silvestre committed suicide. Melilla stood with no Spanish posts between it and Annual, open to attack by Abd el-Krim's victorious troops. The Regulares, still stationed in Melilla, were close to mutiny and panic. In Spain the news of the slaughter at Annual caused a roar of protest against the war in Morocco.

Franco received orders to take on Abd el-Krim. Marching along the path of Silvestre's retreat, Franco's legionnaires saw the litter of dead and dying blocking the road. Franco was horrified and indig-

> We advance rapidly before the enemy can reform. On the way we pass dead Moors. There is a young and pretty Moroccan girl on the field. Her white clothes have over her heart an enormous red stain: her forehead is still warm. Poor little dead child, a victim of war.
> —FRANCISCO FRANCO
> on the violence in Morocco

nant. How could a simple native inflict such an embarrassing defeat on the army of Spain? A desire for revenge took hold of him, and he decided to punish the villages along the route, now occupied by women, children, and elderly men.

Franco recorded the events in his journal: "At midday I got authorization from the general to punish the villages in which the counterattack started and from which the enemy is engaging us. The job is difficult but pretty; . . . while one section opens fire on the houses to cover the maneuver, another slips down by a small cutting, surrounds the villages and puts the inhabitants to the sword; the flames rise from the roofs of the houses and the legionnaires pursue their residents."

Inspired and energized by the bloodletting, the legionnaires wanted to continue advancing. Franco agreed, insisting that there could be no compromise, no negotiations, and that Abd el-Krim had to be defeated and his people destroyed. The legionnaires started their advance in mid-September, but all they could achieve was a stalemate.

Franco conceived a plan for a full-scale landing of Spain-based troops in Alhucemas Bay, about 50 miles west of Melilla, but the government rejected the idea of an invasion. They wanted to reclaim Spanish prestige, but they could not control the dissent at home if more Spanish men died or more money was spent. The troops in Morocco were on their own.

Franco's troops held the ground he had recovered, and things quieted down. On a brief leave, he stopped to see his patient fiancée, Carmen, in Asturias and was honored with a banquet in Oviedo. When he visited El Ferrol, he was greeted by bands, flower-decorated streets, and his proud mother. In most of Spain, though, the massacre at Annual had brought a wave of antiwar sentiment. There were loud demands for a trial for those in the army and government responsible for the defeat. A new governor gave orders to try for a political settlement in Morocco. As government leaders hesitated about the direction they should take, each seeking to shift the blame for the massacre, real power and authority

Moroccan independence leader Abd el-Krim. Even after Primo de Rivera ordered Spanish forces to withdraw to the Moroccan coast, Abd el-Krim continued the attack, seeking to push his enemies into the sea.

began to concentrate in the army. The generals would do as they thought best.

In March 1922 Franco was recalled to Morocco to take part in a new offensive, but the territorial gains were small, and there were many casualties. Franco and his men were ordered to stop their march. On January 12, 1923, Franco was awarded a medal for his service in Africa. Soon afterwards, he left Morocco, believing that if the Spanish Foreign Legion did not get the resources, backing, or permission to win a total victory against Abd el-Krim, there was no point in staying.

Franco rejoined the Prince's Regiment in Oviedo, and rescheduled his wedding for June 15. But on June 5 the new commanding officer of the legion, successor to the hospitalized Millán Astray, was killed. Franco was chosen to take his place. At the age of 30, he was now the youngest lieutenant colonel in the army and commander of the Spanish Foreign Legion. Postponing his marriage again, he bid Carmen good-bye and sailed for Spanish Morocco.

In Franco's absence Abd el-Krim had held the initiative, constantly harassing the hated occupiers of his country. Supplies and ammunition from Spain were almost nonexistent. The various governments appointed by the king could not reach any consistent decisions.

On September 13, 1923, the government's top military advisers, the Military Directory, staged a coup and replaced the Spanish parliament, or Cortes, with military rule. Spain was at that time officially a constitutional monarchy, with parliament holding all power for King Alfonso XIII. The proposed publication of a report on the Annual disaster was canceled, and General Miguel Primo de Rivera pronounced himself dictator, while the king remained titular head of state. Alfonso would soon find himself completely powerless.

Franco was jubilant. Now he would get supplies, fresh troops, and permission to lead a full-scale war against Abd el-Krim. But Primo de Rivera had other plans. Wanting to stay in power in Spain, he decided that Spanish Morocco would have to be sacrificed in order for him to gain popularity with the Spanish people. There simply did not seem to be anyone left in Spain who wanted to hang on to the blood-soaked colony.

"We wish to live in peace with all peoples," Primo de Rivera announced. "We are not imperialists and do not believe that the honor of the army . . . depends on stubborn perseverance in Morocco." He decided that Spain would keep only the major coastal towns and withdraw from the interior.

Franco was outraged by the decision, but he was, as always, obedient to authority. He took a leave of absence and married Carmen in Oviedo on October 22, 1923, taking her on a month-long honeymoon before returning to Spanish Morocco.

But Abd el-Krim was not interested in negotiating away chunks of his land. As long as foreigners had one foot on Moroccan soil, he was determined to fight. Now he made his move to push the Spaniards into the sea. The moment seemed ripe. Spain was war weary. The old and sick leader of the Yebala tribes, Muhammad el-Raisuli, had made peace with the Spaniards, and his angry tribesmen had joined Abd el-Krim's forces. Now there was a strong Moroccan force united under one leader.

In June 1924 the Spanish hold at Tetuán in western Spanish Morocco was threatened. Reinforcements were rushed from the Melilla area and from

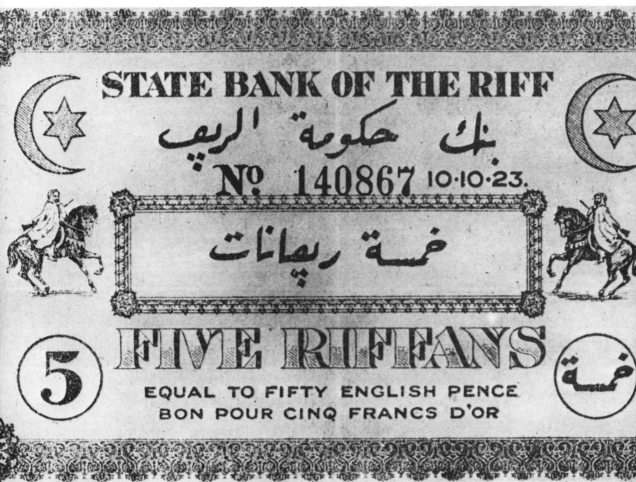

Spain, but the situation was grave. Franco pleaded with the king and Primo de Rivera for a full-scale landing at Alhucemas Bay.

In July Primo de Rivera went to Morocco to observe the situation firsthand. He was greeted at the legion's headquarters with handmade signs reading "The legion never retreats." Franco pleaded emotionally with the dictator, as Primo de Rivera was called: "This soil we tread is Spanish earth, for it has been acquired at the highest price and paid with the dearest money: the Spanish blood that has been shed. . . . We reject the idea of retreating because we are persuaded that Spain is in a position to dominate the zone under her."

Paper currency issued by Abd el-Krim for use by rebel tribesmen of the Riff Mountains in Morocco. In an effort to prove their independence, Moroccan rebels severed all ties with Spain.

Rebel chieftains (foreground) meet at an encampment outside a Moroccan city. Heartened by major victories, Abd el-Krim attacked French forces stationed in French Morocco in 1925. A cooperative French-Spanish counterattack squashed the entire rebel movement.

But Primo de Rivera saw it differently. It was clear that Abd el-Krim and his Moroccan people did not view the Spanish crown as a civilizing force. The dictator ordered Franco to plan for a retreat, and Franco grimly obeyed the order. There were 18,000 casualties during the retreat. The battered survivors reached Tetuán on December 10. Primo de Rivera publicly congratulated the army, but to his associates he acknowledged that: "Abd el-Krim has defeated us. He has the immense advantages of the terrain and a fanatical following. Our troops are sick of the war and have been for years. They don't see why they should die for this strip of worthless territory."

For his obedience, Franco was promoted to full colonel and received the generous gratitude of Primo de Rivera. Nevertheless he continued to argue for a landing at Alhucemas and a final drive to reclaim Morocco. Defeat was something he could not swallow. But Primo de Rivera remained firm. Such a landing would require 200,000 men, and the Spanish people were decidedly against conscription.

In April 1925 events gave Franco his wish. Abd el-Krim, heartened by the defeat and withdrawal of the Spanish army, decided to assist the Beni Zerual tribe against the French in French Morocco, to the south and west of Spanish Morocco. The French government decided to ally themselves with Spain in an effort to put down the rebellion. Primo de Rivera agreed to Franco's plan for a joint landing with the French in Alhucemas Bay, right in the heart of Abd el-Krim's territory.

With General Primo de Rivera himself in command, the first troops ashore were led by Franco and Major José Varela. Franco and his legionnaires annihilated the enemy in a giant attack of retribution for their past defeats. Abd el-Krim and his forces, outnumbered and lacking the massive arms brought in by the French and Spanish, fought hard for their country's independence, but the overwhelming force was too much for them. Many of them were killed, some hurled themselves into the sea from cliffs, and the rest of them finally surrendered. The invading forces had suffered great losses, but Morocco was subdued and would remain in the hands of France and Spain for many years.

It was Franco's last African campaign. At the age of 33, he became the youngest brigadier general in the Spanish army. In a few weeks, Primo de Rivera offered him the chance to head a national army training school.

Franco and his wife left for Zaragoza, in northeastern Spain, to supervise the building and organization of the new school — the General Military Academy — that would bring together the different branches of the Spanish army. The young General Franco believed that he would live peacefully with Carmen, teaching other young men his principles of law and order, discipline and honor. He had no way of foreseeing that in just a few years he would be responsible for a bloodbath that would sweep over Spain and cause moral outrage throughout the world.

> *Franco was now a by-word, almost a legend, among his men as a commander who did not waste lives unnecessarily; among the Regulares who were usually to one or other flank of him, he was regarded as the beloved Allah whom no bullet could touch even when "a sitting target on horseback."*
> —GEORGE HILLS
> British historian

3

Slaughter in Asturias

When his only child, his daughter, Carmen, was born in 1928, it seemed as though Franco was done with war. He carried out his assignment as head of the military academy at Zaragoza with all the diligence he had applied on the battlefields of Morocco. He ran it as a one-man operation with himself as dictator.

But the very existence of the academy depended on General Primo de Rivera's remaining in power. The dictator stayed in control through skillful diplomacy accompanied by a vast amount of luck. At first, all went well. The 1920s was a period of world economic boom, and the royal treasury was amply supplied. The wealthy were happily getting wealthier from government contracts for dams, bridges, and roads. If the poor cried out, Primo de Rivera gave them a handout; if peasant movements erupted, he redistributed some land. But if things went too far, he sent in army troops, outlawed unions, shut down newspapers.

> *Do not forget that he who suffers wins victories, and that to resist and vanquish every day is the school of victory.*
> —FRANCISCO FRANCO
> address at Zaragoza
> military academy

General Franco with his daughter, Carmen. By the time of Carmen's birth in 1928, Franco was established as the head of the military academy at Zaragoza.

UPI/BETTMANN NEWSPHOTOS

In 1929 the Great Depression swept over the United States and Europe. Trade rapidly came to a virtual standstill, and Spain's treasury was soon depleted. Unable to utilize his doling-out technique, Primo de Rivera's popularity evaporated. A determined movement for democratization swept over the country. Ill and tired, Primo de Rivera resigned in January 1930 and fled to Paris, where he died seven weeks later.

King Alfonso XIII saw the futility of trying to assume the government power he had actually lost years earlier. The king was more worried for his own skin. Traditional supporters were forsaking him. The Catholic church had no confidence that he would protect it from the anarchists. The army command, and even his favorite general, Franco, were enraged that he had let Primo de Rivera escape. But no matter how disgruntled he was with the king, Franco was far more incensed at the specter of democracy, which he perceived as an opening to the system he had been taught to hate most of all — communism. As 1930 advanced, Franco found himself facing a tidal wave of support for a republic.

Even some of the most conservative generals, including José Sanjurjo, who had once been the commander of the forces in Morocco, knew which way the wind was blowing and declared their support for a republic. Marchers in the streets, demanding elections, were often led by sections of the armed forces. To make matters worse, at the air force base of Cuatro Vientos, Franco's younger brother, Ramón, became the leader of a rebellion in favor of a republic. It failed, and Ramón fled to Portugal. Less speedy rebels were caught and condemned to death.

In the autumn of 1930, two feuding groups, the Republicans and the socialists, agreed to work together to abolish the monarchy and establish a democratic republic. King Alfonso promised municipal elections, believing that those who supported a republic would never vote along the same lines as the socialists, and the result would be a stalemate.

But as election day approached, only the anarchists spoke against voting for the republic. Since

The shock and exasperation that accompanied the Great
Depression of the late 1920s and 1930s is captured in
this photograph by Dorothea Lange. As national economies throughout the world collapsed, Primo de Rivera
lost control in Spain. In January 1930, he abandoned
the country to a state of anarchy.

45

THE BETTMANN ARCHIVE

Explosives connected to a
clock sit in a woven basket.
Bombs of this type, favored
by the anarchists, were used
often during the fighting
that followed the disso-
lution of Primo de Rivera's
government.

1927 they had gained much influence in the huge
trade union they had organized, the Iberian Anarchist Federation (FAI). The anarchists believed
that a new republic would continue to follow the
dictates of the landowners and industrialists.

The municipal elections produced a Republican
triumph. Franco heard the results in his study at
the military academy on April 14, 1931. People sang
and drank wine in the streets, toasting "la niña
bonita" ("the pretty girl") — the affectionate name
they gave to their new republic of Spain. A few days
later, the king left for Italy, saying that he would
come back when the Spanish people wanted him
again.

There was great relief among the wealthy at the
peacefulness of the change. Many had expected a
revolution and the loss of their vast holdings, but
the provisional government was composed of moderate men. Prime Minister Niceto Alcalá Zamora
(who would be named president of the republic in
December 1931) knew that he faced a difficult, if
not impossible, task. The anarchists would not be
satisfied with promises. They would undoubtedly
continue to organize strikes and carry out acts of
terror.

Additionally, there was the Catholic church,
which wanted to retain its ancient rights and priv-
ileges, its control over thousands of acres of land
and the nation's schools. The people were demanding separation of church and state, which was the
prevailing situation in most of the Western world.
In addition there were the separatists of Catalonia
and the Basque region who were pressing for home
rule. The army officers were split three ways, among
those who gave cautious support to the republic,
those who were firm monarchists, and those, like
Franco, who adopted a wait-and-see attitude.

The new members of government were, for the
most part, idealists — professors, lawyers, poets,
and writers with almost no political experience.
There was no middle class to speak of — only the
very rich or very poor. The rich feared that they
would have to share some of their wealth, and the
poor were afraid that the new republic would vac-

illate and give them little or nothing. In the meantime, the workers of Spain had stopped toasting the republic and were watching and waiting to see what the actions of the new leaders would be.

Most supporters of the republic urged the disbanding of the most hated symbol of the dictatorship, the Civil Guard, which was a paramilitary corps similar to a secret police. The provisional government hesitated to turn police powers over to the popular militias demanded by the people. Instead, it named General Sanjurjo, of Moroccan fame, as commander of the 30,000-strong Civil Guard and even created a separate branch — the *asaltos*, or "assault guards" — specifically to suppress rebellion in the cities. The brutality of the Civil Guard soon increased. In Seville, guardsmen ended a strike by killing 22 workers and wounding 200 others.

Demolished railway cars clog a bridge following the explosion of a bomb set by anarchists. Such violence was the anarchists' method of opposing the creation of a Spanish republic, which they felt would favor the wealthy landowners and industrialists.

A detachment of the Civil Guard fires on Republican supporters in 1932. This corps of secret police, led by General José Sanjurjo, was the feared and hated symbol of dictatorship.

Less than a month after the proclamation of a republic, a group of officers met to plot its overthrow and the return of Alfonso XIII. When a monarchist officer, arriving at the conspirators' house, struck down his taxi driver for shouting "Long Live the Republic," an angry crowd, believing the taxi driver had been killed, stormed through Madrid, setting fire to a monarchist newspaper office and anti-Republican churches. The rioting spread to several Spanish cities. To calm things down, the provisional government scheduled nationwide elections for a national Cortes for June 28, 1931.

The results of the elections were indisputable. The conservatives in the Cortes were swamped by moderate socialists and progressive Republicans. The

Cortes immediately set to work to frame a new constitution for the Spanish Republic. By the following December the Spanish constitution was finalized. It included guarantees that had existed in Western Europe and the United States for decades — equality before the law, universal suffrage, separation of church and state, free and compulsory primary education, protective labor laws.

Some of the new labor laws were enforced, and many new schools were built. These changes, however, were only a fraction of the renovation that was needed. The worst problem was that of land ownership, which remained concentrated in the hands of the few. Millions of Spaniards were impoverished agricultural workers. At daybreak these landless men gathered in the town square, where a hired agent of the local wealthy landowner picked a few of them for the day's work. The slightly better-off tenant farmers slaved over a tiny plot, gave most of their produce to the landowner, and were deeply in debt to local suppliers. The shaky young republic was afraid to antagonize the powerful landowners by carrying out its promised land reform. Week after week fresh disorders broke out, and the hated Civil Guard stepped in to restore calm in its usual ruthless fashion.

In the remote village of Castilblanco, in the hills of Estremadura, a region of western Spain, four Civil Guardsmen were beaten to death when they tried to break up a public meeting of the anarchist National Confederation of Labor (CNT) on December 31, 1931. The violence of the townspeople's reaction alarmed the entire nation. It was an indication of the growing resentment throughout the countryside. A government investigation concluded that the whole village of 900 people had been involved. In Sallent, in the region of Catalonia, members of the CNT drove the Civil Guard from the town, captured the town hall, and declared a free republic. It took government forces five days to recapture the town.

Undoubtedly, Franco was incensed by these disorders, but as long as he headed the military academy he kept silent and obeyed the legal government. But this silence would not last.

Discipline . . . requires its full value when thought counsels the opposite to what we are ordered to do; when the heart swells in inward rebellion against what is ordered: when one knows Authority is wrong and acting out of hand.
—FRANCISCO FRANCO
on the dissolution of the
Zaragoza military academy

Manuel Azaña, a popular liberal leader of the Republican Left party, had been made minister of war in the provisional government. Many people wanted the same fate for the army as for the Civil Guard — turn over the arms to a popular militia to safeguard the new democracy. Instead, Azaña chose the middle road, suspending admission to the academies and reducing the commanding officers of the army to a quarter of their original number through mandatory retirements at full pay. Despite the continued paychecks, many of the officers resented their enforced vacations, and plots to topple the republic multiplied. Franco had kept his distance, hoping that loyalty and obedience would protect his school.

In the spring of 1931, the military academy had been ordered closed. On July 14 Franco had made

"Long Live the Republic," cheer hundreds of railroad workers. The April 1931 proclamation of the republic was greeted by the middle and lower classes with wild enthusiasm across the entire country.

a cautious farewell speech to his cadets and cleared out his office. Still, he bided his time, doing his duty at his new post as commander of an infantry brigade in La Corunna, in his own home region of Galicia, where he was a local hero.

Franco believed that patience would pay off. It was plain that the new government could not last for long, and he believed that when it fell, the rightists (the monarchists and conservatives) would take over, restoring the power of the army. The socialists and anarchists predicted an opposite chain of events — a socialist revolution that would cease to cater to the rich and would finally bring a better life to the poor.

But Franco's old friend José Sanjurjo was not willing to wait. Azaña, attempting to calm down opponents of the Civil Guard, took its leadership away from Sanjurjo and made him chief of customs police. Humiliated by the demotion, in August 1932 Sanjurjo gathered a group of army officers around him to attempt another coup. Aligning themselves with the monarchists and the Church, they distributed arms and attempted to seize control of Seville, planning to move on to the capital city of Madrid after an easy victory. But they underestimated the popular desire for democracy.

The Spanish army parades through Madrid in celebration of the election of Niceto Alcalá Zamora as president of the new republic. A moderate, Alcalá Zamora faced the difficult task of placating the diverse Republican groups.

51

Peasants journey toward the city of Segovia, Spain. Because the economic improvements promised by the republic were slow in coming, rebellions erupted throughout the countryside.

The citizens of Seville were disappointed at the achievements of the republic but had no intention of allowing an army coup. They fought back hard and defeated the insurgents. In Madrid, waiting to take power, Sanjurjo learned that most of the garrisons of conscripted soldiers had proved loyal to the republic. Sanjurjo was caught attempting to flee to the coast and was sentenced to death. Rather than make him a martyr, however, the Republican government put him in prison with common criminals.

Azaña distrusted Franco and so named him commanding officer of the military forces in the remote Balearic Islands, off the eastern coast of Spain. On

March 16, 1933, Franco assumed his new command. He knew that as long as the existing regime controlled the army, the way to the top was denied to him. If the next elections swung to the right, however, perhaps the army would once again be powerful; perhaps his academy would reopen.

Franco did not have long to wait. With the Republican and socialist forces disappointed in the new government, more and more people dropped out of politics and went back to their personal affairs. The mood of the country was swinging to the right. The opponents of the republic saw their chance. From the autumn of 1933 José María Gil Robles, an admirer of the German fascist leader Adolf Hitler, was the head of a new, powerful opposition group. The Catholic Action party, which had appeared in the 1920s, merged with other Catholic groups and conservative landholders to form the Spanish Confederation of the Autonomous Right (CEDA), which then constituted an electoral bloc with the monarchists and other anti-Republican forces. In November 1933 CEDA topped the polls in the general elections, bringing Gil Robles to parliament with 110 deputies.

Azaña's leftist Republicans and the socialists were greatly reduced in number in the Cortes. Alejandro Lerroux's center-right Radical party, supporting neither the Republicans nor the CEDA, finished second. Unwilling to deal with the ultra conservative Gil Robles, President Alcalá Zamora had the aging Lerroux appointed prime minister. Anxious to have the support of Gil Robles's strong CEDA group, Lerroux repealed labor laws, granted amnesty to Sanjurjo and his fellow insurgents (whom he reinstated with back pay), evicted the peasants from lands they had received or seized under the Republican administration, and gave the Church back many of the powers it had lost. It was clear to most Spaniards that the actual power in Madrid was held by a solid bloc of rightist parties led by Gil Robles.

Earlier in October 1933, José Antonio Primo de Rivera, the son of the dead dictator, bent on avenging his father's overthrow and taking power, had organized the Falange, a party with a fascist pro-

José María Gil Robles, leader of the Spanish Confederation of the Autonomous Right (CEDA). When his party was victorious in the 1933 elections, Gil Robles proceeded to repeal the progressive labor laws recently enacted.

53

gram: to control the country by means of force, end individual freedoms, abolish trade unions, and organize military groups.

Now the opponents of the rightist groups woke up to the fact that their fragile democracy was in danger. They stopped their squabbling and joined together in a common cause, preparing for the next elections but also arming themselves in preparation for a possible fascist coup.

In January 1933 a small group of leftist rebels, members of the anarchist FAI, took over the village of Casas Viejas in the province of Cádiz. The army marched in and violently ousted the rebels. There was a wave of popular outrage. After all, the traitor Sanjurjo's life had been spared, but opponents of the rightist groups were murdered. A violent confrontation seemed inevitable. In attics and cellars of leftists and rightists, weapons were collected and young people were trained to use them. Francisco Largo Caballero, a socialist leader who had been arrested during a 1917 rebellion of Asturian miners, toured the country, calling for the workers and peasants to seize power. The center had proven itself unable to preserve the republic, and unless the common people acted, Spain would become a fascist state like Italy, Germany, and Austria.

Youths from the fascist Falange movement on a student exchange in Germany. The Spanish fascist movement was dedicated to controlling Spain through force and ending all liberal organizations.

THE BETTMANN ARCHIVE

In the Balearics in October 1934, Franco learned that the General Workers' Union (UGT), a socialist trade union, had called a general strike in Spain in response to the allocation of three posts in Lerroux's government to right-wing CEDA members. Everything was shut down. Street fighting flared in Madrid, and in Barcelona a full-scale rebellion started. In Catalonia, the region around Barcelona, Luis Companys, the leader of the Catalan nationalists, proclaimed a separate Catalan state and called upon the people to rally against the monarchists and fascists who had betrayed the republic. Martial law and suspension of civil liberties were declared for all of Spain, and troops were hastily dispatched to the region. Twenty people were killed, and Companys and his separatist government were thrown in jail.

It was only the beginning. Gil Robles and his CEDA were ready to move in for the kill. It was time to throw out the constitution and rule Spain with an iron hand. First they would set an example by provoking their toughest opponents — the Asturian miners and their allies.

Gil Robles had held a CEDA convention at Covadonga, in the heart of Asturian mining country, where the rightists had loudly denounced republicanism and the "red miners." The miners responded with a united general strike and formed a new organization of the unified workers of Asturias — Unity of Working-Class Brothers (UHP) — that combined the forces of the socialists, communists, and anarchists. On October 7, 1934, they called on the people of Asturias to revolt against the fascists holding governmental power in Madrid. Setting up an emergency government, they assembled a volunteer army of about 30,000 men from ages 18 to 40, many of them miners, and quickly drilled and trained the new recruits. The army was run as a model of democracy; every officer was elected and the troops showed remarkable discipline and unity.

First the miners seized the government buildings in the area, killing the Civil Guardsmen who had not been wise enough to flee and taking over the radio station in Turón. In Oviedo, a 1,000-man army unit with four colonels and nine majors locked

A day could come, when not only the Republic but the country itself called for him.
—ALEJANDRO LERROUX
prime minister of the
Second Spanish Republic,
on Franco

55

Spanish troops march toward Seville. Due to numerous outbreaks of violence and strikes by the separatists in Catalonia, Gil Robles declared martial law and suspended civil liberties throughout the country.

itself in its barracks when it heard that the miners were coming. Large arms factories were occupied and run by the rebels, who planned to march on Madrid and declare a socialist republic for all of Spain.

In Madrid, Lerroux and Gil Robles could think of only one man who could stop the miners—Francisco Franco. Conveniently, Franco was already in Spain, on leave in Madrid and planning to go to Oviedo so that Carmen could visit her parents and show off their little daughter. Franco, in a strong bargaining position, met with the war minister, Diego Hidalgo. As far as Franco was concerned, events were proving his interpretation of history. Republicanism had weakened the army, and now the government was looking for real soldiers.

Making it clear that he had to write his own ticket, Franco told Hidalgo that there were no forces in Spain that could successfully crush the miners now that they were armed. Only the experienced shock troops from northern Africa could do the job. Furthermore, he wanted tanks and planes to back them up. Hidalgo gave in — knowing full well the reputation of the legionnaires as men lusting for the kill. He feebly extracted a promise from Franco that Spanish lives would be spared.

On October 12 the Spanish Foreign Legion and the Moroccan Regulares, commanded by Colonel Juan Yagüe Blanco, landed at the Asturian port of Gijón and moved swiftly to Oviedo. They screamed their favorite chant, "Long Live Death." Their planes rained bombs on the town, and their tanks stormed toward the miners. For two weeks the miners valiantly fought back. Left with only a few sticks of dynamite, they offered to surrender on the condition that the legionnaires and Regulares withdraw from Asturias. The leaders of the revolt were assured that no reprisals against the workers would be ordered. In their last radio broadcast the revolutionaries told the people of Spain, "Our surrender today is merely a halt on the route . . . which must end in the ultimate victory of the exploited." They had no way of knowing that the halt would last for almost 40 years.

Instead of authorizing the agreement for withdrawal, Franco reinforced his military forces and unleashed them in a month-long systematic terror campaign to wipe out the opposition. More than a thousand Asturian miners were murdered and 30,000 packed into prisons, many of them starving there or dying from cruel tortures and wounds. Women were raped and shot, and even children were not spared. Luis Sirval, a journalist who went to the area to report on the events, was thrown into jail and murdered by three legion officers.

Franco visited the still-smoldering ruins of Oviedo and commented to the press, "The war of Morocco . . . had a certain romantic air, an air of reconquest. But this war is a frontier war, and the fronts are socialism, communism, and any other forms that attack civilization to replace it by barbarism." But throughout the country it was Franco's name that became synonymous with barbarism, fascism, and the death of democracy. In Madrid, though, the right-wing government called Franco and his men saviors of the nation.

In Asturias and the rest of Spain hatred grew tremendously against the leaders who ordered the ruthless extermination of the miners. The Republicans and leftist groups planned revenge. Manuel Azaña had tried to make peace among the rebellious leftists in Barcelona, but he had been arrested as a

Civil Guardsmen keep watch over striking Asturian mineworkers. In October 1934 the mineworkers rose in a bloody revolt, killing members of the local Civil Guard and capturing some regional government installations.

conspirator despite his efforts. In jail he was seen as a hero when it became clear he had been unjustly prosecuted. He was released, along with Largo Caballero, who had also been arrested for inciting rebellion, in December 1934.

For commanding the massacre in Asturias, Franco won the Grand Cross of Military Merit. In February he was made commander in chief of the armed forces in Morocco and sailed off to Ceuta. But he stayed in that Moroccan port city for only three months.

Gil Robles, who had become the government's war minister, appointed Franco chief of the general staff and brought him back to Madrid. Now Franco was in total charge of the army. His plan for a new and modern Spanish army could immediately go into effect. He worked long hours at the war office. A special sector was organized to investigate the political beliefs of recruits and get rid of any who opposed his methods. Arms factories were placed under military control, and employees were forbidden to join organizations on Franco's "red" list, which included unions.

CEDA and Gil Robles were determined to assume control of the government, and in October 1935 Lerroux gave them the excuse to dump him. Relatives and close friends of his were caught in a series of gambling scandals. Gil Robles moved to take power, but the constitution was still in effect, and the constitutional president, Niceto Alcalá Zamora, would not grant the necessary consent. Instead, general elections were scheduled for February 16, 1936. Gil Robles decided to wait it out, confident of victory. The republic still existed, but it hung by a thread. Spain's problems had worsened.

Only Francisco Franco was satisfied. He was one of the most hated men in Spain, but it did not seem to disturb him in the slightest. In his leisure time he hunted rabbits, shopped with Carmen in secondhand furniture stores, and watched Walt Disney cartoons with his family. He stayed away from political meetings, even though he and Gil Robles were still very close. As always, Franco tied his fate to a rising star and broke the bond when the star fell.

AMNISTIA
FRENTE POPULAR
PARA CADA CLIENTE
UNA GORRA DE SU GUST
VOTAD A LAS IZQUI
SOCORRO RO
VOTAD AL BLOQUE POPU

4

"Long Live Death"

All during January 1936 the Spanish people were deeply involved in a wildly partisan election campaign. The massacre in Asturias and Gil Robles's buildup of the army had awakened many disappointed Republicans to the right-wing danger. All who opposed fascism and supported democracy joined together in one common cause — to save the republic.

Republicans, socialists, and communists joined to create the Popular Front coalition. Its program included amnesty for political prisoners and a speedup in reforms, especially reforms dealing with land ownership. The alliance's main objective, however, was to prevent the rightists from gaining power. Since most of the supporters of the Popular Front were poor peasants and workers, the group had only a scrawny campaign treasury.

The rightist groups had also unified for the elections. Their National Front party, a coalition of Robles's CEDA, monarchists, and other right-wing groups supported by wealthy landowners, busi-

We shall preserve what is just: fraternity, liberty and equality. Long live Spain. Long live the Spanish people in honor.
—FRANCISCO FRANCO
from a radio broadcast
aired during the
generals' rebellion

Popular Front election posters adorn a Spanish city wall during the 1936 elections. Running against the powerful, right-wing National Front party, the Popular Front coalition waged a propaganda war in order to wrest control of the Cortes from the rightists.

A nun casts a ballot at an anticommunist center. The Catholic church, a conservative mainstay in Spain, supplied much of the financial backing for the National Front.

nessmen, and the Catholic church, had a huge campaign treasury. It did not publicize its program, but its speeches made it clear: return of the land to the big landowners, restoration of the powers of the Church and the army, and a return to the monarchy. Confident that the National Front would win, Franco went to London to represent Spain at the funeral of Britain's King George V. There he played golf with Britain's elite, learned a little English, and enjoyed mixing with the British nobility. He returned to Spain for election day, February 17.

When the votes were counted, the Popular Front had swept the election. The rightist coalition screamed that the election was illegal, and Nationalists roamed the streets beating up supporters of the republic. But Franco and the Church hierarchy admitted that the Popular Front had won the election.

For the first time, Franco had to face a serious setback. He visited two friends in the early hours of the morning to warn of revolutionary mobs in the streets. Both assured him that the crowds were Republicans rejoicing over their unexpected victory. But Franco was not the only one to panic. Wealthy Spaniards raced from the country, taking their gold and other valuables with them.

A conspiracy had started right after the votes were counted. This time Franco was ready to join ranks with three insurgent generals — Emilio Mola Vidal, Manuel Goded Llopis, and Sanjurjo. With many Catholic conservatives and some of the nation's richest businessmen financing them, Franco believed they could seize power.

When informants told the leaders of the republic that a coup was planned for April 25, José Antonio Primo de Rivera, whose Falangist party had been outlawed by the new regime, was arrested, and key right-wing generals were transferred to remote areas. Goded was shipped off to the Balearics and Franco to the Canary Islands, 800 miles to the southwest of Spain, far from his legionnaires and Regulares.

Before he left in March, Franco went to say his official farewells. He sternly reminded President Alcalá Zamora that the army was now severely weakened, and if a revolution swept the country, it would be difficult to suppress.

Five months after the Popular Front coalition swept the elections, Franco and his fellow generals led a major revolt against the new government (shown here in its first session), commencing the Spanish Civil War.

As fascist troops prepare to invade Barcelona, Republicans stand in defiance behind a barricade. Lacking both arms and training, the Republicans often fought the well-supplied Nationalists with stones and bottles.

"Don't worry, General, don't worry," Alcalá Zamora assured him. "There will be no communism in Spain."

"Of that I am certain," Franco shouted. "And I can answer that whatever contingencies may arise here, wherever I am there shall be no communism."

For weeks the new Cortes was crippled by rioting, rumors, and the blocking of legislation. In May the majority voted to oust Alcalá Zamora from the presidency, finding him guilty of authorizing the slaughter of the Asturian workers by Franco's Moroccan troops. Azaña became president but there was not much he could do to fulfill the Popular Front's election promises.

64

The Popular Front had promised land distribution, and the plowing season had arrived with much land uncultivated. In the absence of government action, peasants in western and southern Spain carried out their own land reform, seizing unoccupied lands. In Madrid, the capital, 70,000 striking construction workers demanded that the government begin to carry out its election promises.

To avoid losing popular support, the Azaña cabinet suspended rent payments in the countryside and declared the occupied lands the legal property of the squatters. They distributed seed, tools, and credit, freed thousands of political prisoners, and restored the powers of the municipal governments. Order was restored, and support for the republic was revived.

On July 13, 1936, José Calvo Sotelo, a deputy who had been making profascist speeches in the Cortes, was assassinated in reprisal for the murder of a popular Republican policeman. National Front members of the Cortes resigned. It was the starting signal for the generals' uprising.

Dolores Ibarruri — "La Pasionara" ("the Passionate One") — on her 80th birthday in 1975. During the Spanish Civil War, Ibarruri made many impassioned radio speeches in defense of the faltering republic.

A Republican soldier holds
aloft a flag to celebrate the
capture of the Guadarrama
Mountains in northern
Spain.

66

The cautious Francisco Franco had staked his whole career on its success, and he was already making plans to rise to the pinnacle of power. He anticipated stiff resistance in Madrid and Barcelona, where the generals would have to utilize half-hearted conscripts, reluctant to shoot their brothers and sisters. He would arrive with his disciplined legionnaires and Regulares, the Army of Africa, and in no more than six weeks, he figured, Spain would be saved and he would be the hero. But first he would have to get from his Canary Island outpost in the Atlantic Ocean to Morocco and transport thousands of men to the Spanish mainland.

The first part of the plan was easy. A pilot was hired in England to bring Franco from the Canary Islands to Morocco, and the Nationalists took over both colonies easily. Spain would be more difficult.

In Madrid the government belatedly sent three destroyers to Morocco and announced that Franco, Goded, Mola, and Sanjurjo were dismissed from the army as traitors — by then a mere formality. The one thing that would have helped save the republic — arming the populace — remained undone. Only the armed forces in Spain had weapons, and it could be anticipated that many of them would join the Nationalist generals. But the Republican government was fearful of armed workers and peasants and announced that anyone who gave out weapons would be executed.

While radio stations blared out the reassuring news that the plot was confined to the colonies, the Nationalists were moving rapidly to take over Spain. Nationalist army units used terror and surprise against unarmed populations. General Gonzalo Queipo de Llano took Seville on July 17, 1936. Smearing his men with walnut juice to make them look like Moroccans, he made terrorist raids by truck into several working-class neighborhoods. Searching house to house and seizing all the males, he then began a series of public executions in the main square. In the early days of August alone, 7,000 people were executed. Queipo de Llano bragged on the radio that the insurgents had "struck the word 'pity' out of their dictionary."

In Cádiz, Granada, and Córdoba there was street fighting, but the supporters of the republic had only sticks, stones, and bottles, while the Nationalists had rifles and grenades. Refugees from Granada told the press of thousands butchered there. Journalists who tried to tell the outside world the horrors of these events were often murdered as well.

Franco wholeheartedly backed these measures. At Tetuán a reporter asked him how long the massacre would go on. Franco replied, "There can be no compromise, no truce. . . . I shall save Spain from Marxism at whatever cost."

"And if that means that you will have to shoot half of Spain," the reporter pressed on.

"I repeat, at whatever cost."

The Nationalists were defeated only in cities and towns where local officials distributed arms to the citizens. In Barcelona the principal squares and public buildings were seized by troops led by General Goded, but the workers retook the city and captured Goded.

On July 18 a group of young officers and aviators, loyal to the republic, distributed almost 5,000 rifles to workers and led them to the airfields and barracks of Madrid to stop the uprising. That night Dolores Ibarruri, a communist deputy, made her first radio appeal to the Republicans. "It is better to die on your feet than to live on your knees! *No pasarán!* [They shall not pass!]" her voice rang out over loudspeakers all over the capital. She would be called *La Pasionaria*, the passionate one, for her inspiring speeches in defense of the republic.

On the morning of July 20, 1936, huge crowds chanted "Arms! Arms! Arms!" outside the war ministry in Madrid. Inside everyone was telling Azaña that the only chance of defeating the rebellion was to arm the workers. At last he gave the order to distribute weapons.

Chanting "Death to Fascism" and "Long Live the Republic," thousands of civilians raced off to storm the Montaña barracks. They hung the resisting officers and captured their rifles and ammunition. All of them armed now, they marched off to help their brothers in the neighboring cities of Toledo and

Here you have it. It is the one which belongs to you . . . which they tried to rob from you . . . this is our flag, on which we all swore, for which our fathers died . . . the flag a hundred times covered with glory.
—FRANCISCO FRANCO
unfurling the old red and gold flag of the monarchy as the symbol of Nationalist Spain

Guadalajara. These untrained, armed people were the first victorious columns of what became known as the Loyalist Militia — common citizens defending democracy. Elsewhere, despite heroic resistance, the insurgents rapidly took over almost a third of Spain.

In Morocco, Franco was getting one cable after another. There would be no fleet to take him and the Army of Africa to the mainland. Sailors loyal to the republic had refused to allow their officers to sail the needed ships to Morocco. Sanjurjo had died in a plane crash, and Goded had been captured in Barcelona. Now Franco's only competitor for leadership of the uprising was Mola, who was in a good strategic position inside Spain to command the action, while Franco remained stranded in Morocco.

In the central northern province of Burgos on July 23, Mola proclaimed a provisional government of the

Nationalist soldiers rest after a battle. The Nationalists quickly gained control over large areas of Spain while Franco remained stranded in Morocco, desperately seeking transportation to Spain for his army.

Hermann Goering, commander of Nazi Germany's Luftwaffe (air force). Goering convinced Hitler to send planes to transport Franco and his troops to Spain and subsequently conducted devastating bombing raids against Republican outposts.

Nationalists. Upstaged and impatient, Franco desperately searched for transportation for his army. He had sent representatives to Benito Mussolini in Rome and Adolf Hitler in Berlin, appealing to them for transport planes, and at last he received a response.

Mussolini, anxious to test his war materials, agreed to send aid from Italy to the insurgents. Hermann Goering, chief of the *Luftwaffe*, the German air force, convinced Hitler that it was necessary to aid Franco, "first, to prevent the further spread of communism; second, to test my young Luftwaffe in this or that technical respect." Half a million Spaniards would be the human guinea pigs in that test of the world's first full-scale bombings of civilian populations.

The airplanes arrived on July 30, 1936, and Franco began airlifting his troops across the Straits of Gibraltar. But the process was maddeningly slow. The Germans next sent two battleships and a torpedo boat, destroyed a Republican battleship, picked up hundreds of Army of Africa troops and took them across the straits. With roaring war planes flying overhead, no one could stop them. In British-held Gibraltar the authorities allowed the ships to refuel, although they had refused to sell fuel to the Republican navy. In deed if not word, Britain was aiding Hitler, Mussolini, and Franco.

From the earliest days of the Spanish Civil War, outside help, or lack of it, was the determining factor on both sides. The Republicans were terribly short of arms and equipment and received little or no help from the Western democracies — Great Britain, France, the United States. The leaders of those countries were afraid of antagonizing Hitler and Mussolini.

British businessmen aided the Nationalists, and American companies sold them oil and trucks. Léon Blum, the socialist premier of France, convinced the major European powers to join in a nonintervention agreement, a pact establishing that neither side in the civil war would get help. France generally obeyed the agreement, but Germany and Italy did not.

Hitler and Mussolini sent more and more men and materials to the Nationalists. They thought a fascist Spain would be helpful to them in their plans to conquer Europe. The Soviet Union, terrified of a fascist Europe, sent arms and equipment to the pro-republic loyalists but also participated in the signing of the nonintervention pact.

Early in August, Franco and 20,000 of his elite troops landed on the southern coast of Spain and marched into the Seville region, where one of his allies, General Queipo de Llano, held power. As Franco, Queipo de Llano, and Millán Astray stood

To whomsoever feels a sacred love for Spain. . . . The situation is becoming more critical every day. . . . Can we consent one day longer to the shameful spectacle we are presenting to the world?
—FRANCISCO FRANCO
from a radio broadcast
aired July 18, 1936

71

Léon Blum, socialist premier of France in 1936. Believing that Spain should solve its own internal problems, Blum engineered the signing of a nonintervention agreement among the nations of Europe. France observed the pact, but Italy and Germany did not.

on the balcony of the Seville town hall overlooking their Nationalist command center, Queipo de Llano bragged that "Madrid will be ours in a few days. . . . The rabble must surrender or be shot like dogs."

Remaining in Seville, Franco commanded battles by radio. Now he wanted leadership, not battles that could endanger his life. His friend Colonel Yagüe led truckloads of Army of Africa men rapidly north. The bloody story repeated itself everywhere. At the old walled town of Badajoz, where the largest peasant land seizures had taken place, the people resisted bitterly. On August 14 newsmen watched as Badajoz's militia mounted machine guns on the city walls. The fascists dynamited the city gates and attacked the machine-gun posts from the rear, capturing the town. Then, right in front of newsmen, Yagüe executed the militiamen and ordered the rest of the townspeople into a bullring, where the Regulares and legionnaires mowed them down in a hail of machine-gun fire.

Later, Franco commented to a journalist that he saw "no inconsistency in killing peasants for their own good or in eliminating opposition through murders masked as military executions."

At the end of August, to oversee the conquest of Madrid, Franco went to Cáceres, about 150 miles southwest of the capital, and established his head-

A French crowd cheers a leftist election victory. Though France officially steered a neutral course during the Spanish Civil War, the majority of French people emphatically supported the Spanish Republic's cause.

quarters in an elaborate palace. At his side was his brother Nicolás, called disparagingly "the general's butler." Once, Nicolás had outshone his younger brother, but now he was a mere aide, arranging imports of armaments from Portugal.

By early September the fascist armies were advancing on the nation's capital. Franco announced his intent: "Marxist rabble, the sons of La Pasionaria, can count their days numbered in Madrid." Only a unified defense could save the city. But unity among the loyalists, who believed in democratic decision making, was not easy.

In the Nationalist zones differences of opinion were forbidden; the rebels ruled through official terror and martial law. Strikes were outlawed, land reforms were nullified, and priests, civil servants, and businessmen cooperated. Labor leaders and militiamen were herded into overcrowded, hellish prisons. Village purge committees were established — composed of a priest, a member of the Civil Guard, and the local landowner. If all three condemned the prisoner, he was executed.

Status or fame meant nothing. On August 19, 1936, the world-famous poet and dramatist from Andalusia, Federico García Lorca, had been executed without a trial. The fascists referred to these acts as the "land reform," whereby the *rojo separatistas* (red separatists) would finally get their "piece of land."

Among the loyalists there were two sharply different strategies proposed for defending the republic. The Azaña forces, which included liberals, some socialists, and communists, called for wartime unity of all democratic forces, even if this meant postponing reforms.

But in Catalonia and a few other areas where anarchists, socialists, and communists of the Workers' Party of Marxist Unification (POUM), formed in 1935, had the most influence, the people were willing to risk their lives only if they had real changes to defend. Jails were opened and political prisoners were freed. All symbols of privilege — even fancy hats and ties — disappeared from the streets. Women disdained the laws of fashion and wore slacks. Infor-

Federico García Lorca, renowned poet and dramatist. García Lorca was one of the many liberal thinkers executed during the fascists' purge trials held throughout the Nationalist-occupied regions.

British author George Orwell. Although he went to Spain as a journalist, Orwell joined the Catalonia-based POUM militia to fight the Nationalists. Orwell's *Homage to Catalonia* describes the conflict in the besieged mountain region of northern Spain.

mation on birth control was distributed, and divorce was permitted. The homes of the wealthy who had fled the country and churches abandoned by fascist priests were used for schools, orphanages, or clinics. Thousands of people received free health care. Factories were taken over by the workers, and wages were raised. Rents, food prices, and electric and gas costs were all lowered.

The leaders were making Catalonia a model of the egalitarian society they had preached about. Similar steps were being taken in Valencia, parts of Madrid, Asturian mining towns, and many Mediterranean ports. In the countryside, the Civil Guard reigned no longer. Inequality was abolished, and property ownership records were destroyed. Municipal governments ruled democratically, with one representative from each party of the Popular Front.

The Communist party called this an "infantile, premature, revolution." To please the Soviet Union, or rather its leader, Joseph Stalin, the communists wanted the anarchists and anti-Stalinist POUM members, who were critical of the lack of democracy in the Soviet Union, eliminated from the antifascist coalition. Soviet freighters received orders not to unload in anarchist and POUM-controlled Barcelona. Worse yet, assassinations between the factions of the left began.

As a move to satisfy everyone, on September 4, Francisco Largo Caballero was named prime minister. As the head of the socialist General Workers' Union (UGT), he had the loyalty of organized labor and knew how to cooperate with the communists and anarchists. The people trusted him to preside over the defense of Madrid. In the eyes of Franco and the insurgents, the addition of Caballero to the government meant that the "red conquest" had taken place.

Madrid was unprepared to defend itself — a plum for Franco to pluck — but its capture would have to wait. Franco wanted first to send aid to Toledo. At the old Alcázar fortress there, Colonel José Moscardó had been barricaded since late July with his troops, their families, and over a hundred Republican hostages. Moscardó's men had plenty of arms

> *We must have looked like something out of a circus because what we found were Moorish daggers, antique swords, and hunting knives. I was one of the last to enter and all I could get was a lance. Can you imagine going off to war with a lance?*
> —a Toledo youth on the loyalist Republicans' arms shortage

but, by the end of August, no food. The fortress and its starving women and children had become a focal point for the news media all over the world.

Making a desperate stand to hold the city at the Toledo cemetery on September 27, hundreds of loyalist militiamen died before a hail of bullets from Franco's advancing army. Franco's hordes then moved on to the barracks and the hospital, where they murdered doctors, nurses, and 400 wounded lying in their beds. Two days later Franco arrived from his safe position behind the front lines and staged the release of the skeletal occupants of the Alcázar for the news cameras.

The fortress of Alcázar in Toledo lies in ruins, September 1936, after Franco's Army of Africa relieved Colonel José Moscardó's Nationalist forces there.

UPI/BETTMANN NEWSPHOTOS

Franco flew to Salamanca, where he met with the other generals to determine who would lead the state. On October 1, 1936, he announced to the cheering monarchists and Nationalists that he was generalissimo (supreme commander of the armed forces) as well as chief of state, with supreme authority over all Nationalist activities. General Mola protested bitterly that Franco had violated the earlier agreement, and a compromise was arranged. Franco would be called "head of state" rather than "chief of state"—essentially a matter of semantics.

Franco's grandstand play at Toledo on September 27 had elevated him to supreme commander, but it

had also given Madrid more time to prepare. On October 7, German bombers pounded at the city's residential neighborhoods as Franco's army made the slow return journey to the north, harassed by anarchist guerrilla units.

On November 7, 1936, General Mola's 20,000 men hurled themselves at the militia that was blocking entry to Madrid. Mola bragged to newsmen, "In 48 hours, gentlemen, I'll treat you to coffee on the Gran Via." Largo Caballero, attempting to bring everyone together for an all-out defense of Madrid, added the anarchists to his coalition government and then fled with his cabinet to Valencia, leaving an older general, José Miaja Menant, to surrender the city.

But the people of Madrid were not about to surrender. They set up barricades, soup kitchens, clinics, and communication centers. Fifteen thousand of them dug in and occupied trenches around the university, at the edge of the city.

On November 8, the Nationalists, led by General José Varela, attacked the university section of Madrid. German planes bombed the defenders. In the streets, the chants of "No pasarán" and "Madrid shall be the tomb of fascism" were shouted day and night as the people listened to the nearby sounds of battle. Their shouts sounded like the echoes of doom. No matter how determined they were to beat back the invaders, it seemed impossible.

Then 3,000 uniformed and helmeted men came marching down Madrid's main avenue. To the cheers of the populace, some jumped into trenches with the militiamen, and the rest paraded on to the wooded edges of the city. They were the first volunteers of the International Brigades, men from all over the world who had come to help stem the tide of fascism. For days, the fierce battle raged, but the arrival of the International Brigades was a turning point.

Franco abandoned the idea of a direct assault on Madrid. He decided instead to keep up the bombings and cut off the main roads to the capital, encircling it. The first Americans arrived in Spain almost two months after the Republican victory. It would be the job of the American volunteers to prevent the fas-

General and fellow Generals. You can be justly proud. You took over a broken Spain. You hand over to me a Spain united in a single great ideal. Victory is on our side. . . . I shall not fail. I shall take the Motherland to her summit, or die in the attempt.
—FRANCISCO FRANCO
on investing himself
as generalissimo and
Nationalist Spain's
head of state

cists from completing their circle. On January 8, 1937, after only a few days of training, they jumped into trucks and headed for the Madrid-Valencia highway, in the Jarama River valley.

Their commander was Robert Hale Merriman, 28 years old, the son of a lumberjack. He had been the star end on the football team at the University of Nevada and had served in the U.S. Reserve Officers Training Corps. It was not much preparation, but it was more than some others had.

Forty-five trucks carrying almost 500 men of the newly named Abraham Lincoln Battalion rolled toward their first battle. They had been issued old World War I rifles, still coated in packing grease. Merriman called a halt to the trucks, and the men all jumped out and fired five practice rounds into the hillside. Stopping to eat, they were attacked by Nationalist planes, which tore up the soil with bombs and machine-gun bullets. But minutes later

A Spanish child's sketch of the Luftwaffe's merciless bombing of homes, schools, and hospitals. The October 1936 German bombing campaign of Madrid was a particularly ruthless one, aiming to destroy residential areas of the city.

81

Republican planes swept across the sky to chase the Nationalists. The Americans cheered as two German planes dropped in flames to the ground.

From February 23 to February 27, the Abraham Lincoln Battalion had its baptism in battle, launching attacks against the Army of Africa to prevent them from taking the highway. Even with their antiquated weapons and lack of artillery they stopped Franco's men. Of the 500 who had started out, 120 were killed and 175 were wounded.

The daily bombings of Madrid continued, but the war was bogged down. The Germans and Italians worried over the events in Spain. They did not want to be stalemated in a civil war there. Franco's inability to take Madrid made them think about replacing him with Mola. Under pressure, Franco accepted a 10-man Italian advisory staff.

In March, without consulting Franco, the Italian "advisers" sent 50,000 Italian troops to capture Guadalajara, close to Madrid. Outnumbered, the antifascist Italians of the Garibaldi International Brigade routed them. From that day forward no adviser questioned Franco's authority.

Growing fat, with his hair turning gray, at 44 Franco stayed close to his castle, strolling in the gardens, preparing to rule Spain. First he ordered a special organization to compile a list of "red criminals." When they finished, Franco had a "Most Wanted" list of 2 million. Then, imitating Hitler, he ordered that all "leftist" books "be destroyed as a matter of public health" and that the political parties supporting him unite in one organization under his control.

Because the majority of the Basque Catholics in northern Spain were fighting to defend the republic, the Vatican had still not given official recognition to the Nationalist government. Franco decided to circumvent Madrid and capture the Basque provinces.

On April 26, 1937, a German bombing campaign was launched to "soften up" the Basques. In the small town of Guernica, the ancient capital of the Basque republic, German fliers carried out Hermann Goering's orders. Guernica provided ideal

UPI/BETTMANN NEWSPHOTOS

Ernest Hemingway, cele-
brated American author, wit-
nessed much of the fighting
in the Spanish Civil War. In
For Whom the Bell Tolls
Hemingway portrayed the
struggle of an American volunteer in war-torn Spain.

83

UPI/BETTMANN NEWSPHOTOS

Orphans rest behind the Nationalist lines in Guernica. In 1937 Franco began a campaign to capture the Basque region of northern Spain. German bombs launched a devastating attack on the small town of Guernica.

"laboratory" conditions for testing the kill ratios of explosive versus incendiary (fire-producing) bombs.

The bombing started in the afternoon when virtually the whole town was at the market in the town square. In minutes the square was turned into a flaming pile of screaming men, women, and children. More than 1,600 were killed and 900 were wounded. The act was so savage that a wave of international protest swept the world, enough to embarrass Franco. He announced that the town had been burned by retreating "reds," but there were too many witnesses for him to get away with the lie. The horrible images of hundreds of people blown up in the streets of a small city could not be erased, even though Franco made it a crime in Spain to mention the bombing of Guernica.

In Barcelona the debate heated up again among the loyalists on the best way to defeat the fascists — with or without a simultaneous social revolution. In early May 1937 Barcelona's political struggle became a civil war within a civil war when the POUM threw its support to the anarchist CNT against a combined socialist-communist group. The same men who had fought together against the insurgents murdered each other. POUM supporters and anarchists all over Catalonia prepared to march to Barcelona to defend their brothers. On May 5 a fragile peace was negotiated, but the Communist party (under Moscow's direction) remained determined to liquidate the anti-Stalinist leadership in the POUM.

In Valencia (to where, in November 1936, the Republican government had retreated), Communist party delegates began to demand that the government outlaw the POUM. Prime Minister Largo Caballero came under tremendous pressure to unify the socialist and communist parties, thereby increasing the communist power base, but he continued to refuse. When the communists (supported by the moderate socialists) stormed out of a cabinet meeting on May 13, Largo Caballero's government fell apart, and he was forced to resign. On May 17 Dr. Juan Negrín, a moderate socialist and a man the communists felt they could easily control, became the new prime minister.

In June 1937 the Nationalists launched an invasion of the Basque country. The Basques had over 50,000 trained militiamen and had placed what they considered to be an iron ring around their capital, Bilbao. Arrayed against them were 50,000 Spanish, Moroccan, and Italian fascists and an incredible arsenal of war machinery. On June 12 armored divisions supplied by the Nazis pierced the Basque defenses, and a week later, after the Basque defenders had been ordered to evacuate the capital, the Army of Africa marched into the city. Those who could not flee were the victims of a savage onslaught of revenge. More than 1,000 people were executed, and 11,000 were jailed.

In the comfort of his home, Franco got the news of victory as well as another pleasing piece of news.

Pale with anger, he said, 'I will not have war made on my own people.'
—a member of Franco's general staff describing Franco's reaction to the bombing of Guernica

The painting entitled *Guernica* by Spanish artist Pablo Picasso captures the pain and suffering of the townspeople. Franco was stung by the intensity of the international protest over Guernica and tried to blame the communists for the town's destruction.

General Mola had been killed in an airplane accident in early June. Not only was Franco the wartime head of state, but his competition was gone. To make matters even better, after the victory in Bilbao the Vatican gave its public support to the fascist cause in Spain. In October Pope Pius XI appointed a papal legate (representative) to Spain.

With the loss of the Basque province, Negrín decided to launch a Republican offensive to take back territory in the south and lift the blockade on Madrid. Again, the International Brigades played a leading role in fierce battles against overwhelming odds. The Abraham Lincoln Battalion won territory

at Brunete, Teruel, and many other towns, but at a great cost in lives.

Despite their victories, most Republicans knew they were being worn down by bombs, hunger, and the lack of help from the outside. The fascists seemed ever stronger, their supplies limitless.

In early 1938 Franco decided to end the war with one big offensive. Among his ranks were some who wanted to offer peace, but Franco insisted on the total humiliation of those who opposed him. Negrín continued to insist on resistance, offering to surrender only if there were free elections, the release of all political prisoners, and agrarian reform.

Ramón Franco, General Franco's younger brother. Exiled in 1930 after leading a doomed Republican revolt, he returned years later to command a Nationalist base on the Mediterranean island of Majorca.

Franco's reply was to order the bombing of Barcelona — a prelude to his decision to overrun and destroy Catalonia and the egalitarian movement he so hated. Ramón Franco, the "naughty boy" of the family, had returned from the United States and quietly became chief of the Nationalist air base at Majorca, a Mediterranean island about 150 miles off the coast of Spain.

All through the first half of 1938 waves of Ramón's bombers took off from Majorca, armed with the latest German aerial weaponry. It was clearly a terror bombing campaign, without even a pretense of aiming for military objectives. France protested, and even the Vatican informed Franco of its displeasure, but Franco told them that Barcelona was jammed with "red" supplies. Ramón Franco himself was killed in the summer of 1938 when his seaplane crashed off Majorca's coast.

While Barcelona was under siege, a fascist land offensive swept through Spain, quickly capturing new territory. In April and May the French frontier was opened again, and war supplies were rushed to the Republicans. On the night of July 24, 1938, the Republicans launched a bold offensive at the Ebro River, an area held by General Yagüe's Moroccan army. Surviving repeated air bombings and strafing runs, they managed to cross the river. Once across, however, the Republicans and the international volunteers were cut to ribbons, many of them drowning in the bloody waters of the Ebro. They called it the "Valley of Death," and one young American from the Abraham Lincoln Battalion described it in his diary: "Place stank with dead. . . . Men dead by hundreds." Franco ordered tens of thousands of his troops into the battle — and nearly 35,000 of them perished.

Winter was coming, and the Germans urged Franco to negotiate peace while he was so clearly the victor throughout Spain. Franco refused. "Criminals and their victims cannot live together," he told the German ambassador.

In March 1938 Hitler occupied Austria, and Premier Léon Blum's Popular Front coalition was returned to power in France. The hopes of the

Republicans surged. If Great Britain and France stopped appeasing Germany and Italy, Spain would become part of a stronger combination of antifascist nations. Socialist representatives flew to Paris and convinced Blum to open the border for the flow of Soviet supplies.

When Hitler began to demand the surrender of Czechoslovakia, the loyalists thought that they could finally join in a common cause with the Western democracies against the fascists. But instead, on September 30, 1938, the leaders of Great Britain, France, Germany, and Italy met at Munich, Germany, and signed the Munich Pact, delivering Czechoslovakia to Hitler.

The Munich Pact was the death blow to the Spanish Republic. The wife of British Prime Minister Neville Chamberlain added insult to injury. Lady Chamberlain toured the Nationalist-held areas of Spain, cementing relations with the fascists. When the press asked her if she intended to visit the Republican areas as well, she said that she could "see no reason" to do so.

At the end of September 1938, those men of the International Brigades who were not dead or in prison were ordered to return home. The Nonintervention Committee, which had been founded in 1936 in an attempt to confine the fighting to Spain alone, had announced a ban on recruitment of non-Spanish soldiers on February 20, 1938, and the Republicans obeyed, hoping that the German, Portu-

Franco observes his Army of Africa march to Barcelona in 1938. With the victory over the Basques in the north, only the eastern region of Catalonia remained beyond the Nationalists' grasp. Franco decided to capture the area in one last, huge offensive.

guese, and Italian fascist troops would withdraw as well. The German and Italian fascists stayed.

On December 23, 1938, Franco launched a final offensive against Catalonia. The Republicans' 220,000 defenders faced 350,000 attackers. Thousands of Spaniards raced for the French border as planes bombed and strafed them along the road. Yagüe's troops occupied the bombed-out city of Barcelona on January 26, 1939. In Valencia the Republican cabinet retreated to Figueras, the last town on the road to France. Negrín held his last Cortes meeting on February 1, 1939, just a few days before the Republican leaders crossed the border. Although the fighting around Madrid continued, Spain now virtually belonged to Franco.

On February 13 Franco announced the Law of Political Responsibilities. Under this decree, if those who had fled came back, they would face trial and possible execution. In late February and March, 400,000 decided to stay in France, and 70,000 chose repatriation. Negrín and the Communist party leaders, safe in France, insisted on continuing the resistance in Madrid and other areas until they got some guarantee against political reprisal. Azaña urged them to concede. Negrín flew to the central war zone and was told that the Republican militia could not fight on.

The final pocket of resistance, Madrid fell to the Nationalists in April 1939. Republicans were rounded up and often executed after Franco became the absolute ruler of Spain.

By 1939 the battle for Madrid had been a stalemate for three long years. But on March 26 the Nationalists launched a final offensive to capture this last Republican-controlled city. The weary, disheartened Republican garrisons in the central and southern zones quickly surrendered, and Madrid was occupied. On April 1, 1939, the Spanish Civil War ended in a complete and unconditional victory for General Franco. On that same day, the United States recognized the new Nationalist government of Francisco Franco.

Every year on April 1, until Franco's death in 1975, the anniversary of a victory in a war Franco called the "Crusade" and the "War of Liberation" took place in Madrid. It celebrated Franco's rise to power over the corpses of more than 600,000. Mass executions from 1936 to 1944 took the lives of another 400,000. An equivalent number fled Spain, becoming refugees in several other countries.

The Spanish Republic was dead, but the world would never forget the butchery caused by the man who made "Long Live Death!" his movement's motto.

The people of Barcelona greet Franco's victorious troops in front of a poster of their new leader. Nationalist troops occupied a bombed-out Barcelona in January 1939.

5

Long Dark Night of Power

Franco rode into Madrid on a white horse on March 28, 1939, cheered by supporters who had hidden during the fight for Madrid. Members of the International Brigades had gone home or were buried with the rest of the dead Republicans. Spanish refugees had filled hastily constructed French camps, surrounded by barbed wire. When France fell to the Nazis in 1940, many were returned to Spain for execution, including Largo Caballero.

Those who stayed in France or made it to Mexico could not cause Franco real trouble. Those who had not escaped Spain were in hiding, and Franco quickly launched a terror campaign to wipe them out. Tens of thousands of veterans of the Republican army were shot or given prison terms of 20 to 30 years. Trade unions and all political organizations of the Republican era were outlawed. The press was controlled, and all the republic's reforms were canceled. In 1941, two years after the end of the civil war, there were still 140,000 political prisoners in Spain.

Those people who urge me to go in with Germany are all wrong, quite wrong. The English will never give in. They'll fight and go on fighting: and if they are driven out of Britain, they'll carry on the fight from Canada: they'll get the Americans to come in with them. Germany has not won the war.
—FRANCISCO FRANCO
after the fall of France
in 1940

General Franco on April 1, 1959, the 20th anniversary of the Nationalist victory in the Spanish Civil War. Once in power Franco instituted a series of repressive measures designed to consolidate his control over Spain, including press censorship, abolition of labor unions and political groups, and repeal of Republican reforms.

Supporters of the Abraham Lincoln Battalion welcome the freedom-fighting volunteers back to the United States. The U.S. government, however, viewed the returning soldiers with suspicion as communist sympathizers.

I remembered the breakfasts of the past, the smell of toast and coffee, the butter spread thick. I belong to a generation which really stopped eating in 1936 and went hungry for ten years.
—Spanish citizen on the famine in Spain

Nor did Franco fear Great Britain or the United States. Both democracies had rushed to recognize Franco's regime even before the Republicans had surrendered.

But Spain's economy was ruined. A disastrous crop failure in 1941 brought Spain to the brink of starvation. Misinterpreting the problem, Franco froze prices at 1936 levels, an action that only served to create a huge black market with prices that only the wealthier Spaniards could afford. The people were exhausted and hungry. All they wanted was a life free of war, no matter who ran the government.

Franco made the luxurious El Pardo Palace his family residence. Fourteen miles north of Madrid, the estate included a full oak forest, stocked with deer for his shooting pleasure. A swimming pool, a tennis court, and a golf course were added. The interior of the former 16th-century palace was extensively renovated.

Trusting no one, Franco surrounded his home with armed guards and seldom ventured off his estate. He was rarely seen in public. When he had to travel, he rode in a Rolls-Royce, surrounded by motorcycle and cavalry escorts.

Six months after the end of the Spanish Civil War, in September 1939, World War II began. On one side were the Axis powers: Germany, Italy, and Japan;

and on the other side were the Allies: Great Britain and France. Later, after they were attacked, the United States and the Soviet Union joined the Allies.

It was during the next six years of the war that Franco's talent as a politician emerged. Not convinced that Hitler and Mussolini would win the war, he was determined to keep Spain out of the conflict. If the Allies won and he was in league with the Axis forces, he was sure to lose power.

But keeping Spain out of World War II was not easy. Hitler and Mussolini had contributed enormously to Franco's victory. Now they wanted him to pay them back by allowing German arms and troops to cross Spain and attack the British in Gibraltar. They pressured Franco to become a full partner in the war.

Franco's reply could produce dire consequences for his country. Spain was on the verge of famine and needed outside food sources. Hitler and Mussolini were busy feeding their own troops, so Franco hoped he could get grain and oil from the United States and the other Allies. Rather than giving Hitler a firm answer, he replied that Spain would indeed join the war, sometime in the future. On the other hand, Franco had to convince the Allies that he would stay neutral if they sent him supplies.

Loyalists of the Spanish Republic flee to France to escape persecution under Franco's Nationalist regime. Thousands who did not manage to escape were shot or imprisoned by the fascists.

Franco most likely hoped for an Axis victory. At the beginning of the war he had two autographed photos on his desk — of Hitler and Mussolini. He gave the two dictators what aid he could without cutting ties with the Allies. When Germany invaded France in the spring of 1940, he wrote to Hitler, "I would like to offer you the expression of my enthusiasm and admiration."

Spain's neutrality required careful diplomacy, and Franco had to maneuver without error. After all, one fatal error and the Allies might consider him a belligerent and occupy Spain, bringing with them an army of vengeful Republicans.

Finally, Hitler insisted on a conference with Franco. On October 23, 1940, they met on the French border at Hendaye, in the German leader's private railway car. Franco deliberately arrived an hour late to throw Hitler off balance. "I'll have to use every trick I can," Franco told one of his senior officers, "and this is one of them. If I make Hitler wait, he will be at a psychological disadvantage from the

A young Spanish refugee accepts food from a French soldier. For those still in Spain, a disastrous harvest in 1941 brought many people to the brink of starvation.

start." For hours Hitler spoke to Franco, demanding that he allow German tank divisions and paratrooper units to pass through Spain and take the British port at Gibraltar to block Allied access to the Mediterranean Sea and northern Africa. In reply, Franco made demands for enormous amounts of food. He alternated between flattering the German leader in his soft, high-pitched, singsong voice and remaining calm and silent while Hitler ranted and raved.

Despite threats and pressures, Franco managed to continue his neutral diplomacy throughout the war. At the beginning of 1941 Hitler sent him a threatening note: "I must deeply regret your views and your attitude. . . . We three men, il Duce [Mussolini], you and I, are linked together by the most implacable force of history. . . . The world's most tremendous military machine [stands ready] . . . and the future will show how good and reliable that instrument is."

Franco told Hitler's emissaries that he agreed with everything Hitler said but that first he must keep a

A Nazi flag flutters as German warplanes fly overhead. Having learned successful bombing tactics during the Spanish Civil War, the German Luftwaffe proved far superior to the Allied air forces in the initial stages of World War II.

97

A Church official in a white hood and robe and a Nationalist army officer lead a religious procession. Although critical of Franco's terror campaign against the Republicans, the Catholic church continued to support his regime.

date to meet Mussolini on February 12. The two got along like old friends. In his journal, Franco made a note of the discussion: "He was honest with me . . . he was very human, natural. Besides, I think I can say he felt friendly towards me. . . . 'Duce,' I said, 'if you could get out of the war, would you?' He burst out laughing and, throwing his arms into the air, cried out: 'You bet your life I would.' "

Following the meeting, Mussolini sent a letter to Germany informing Hitler that Spain was in no condition to enter the war. Hitler ranted to his advisers of Franco's ingratitude, "cowardly defection," and "underhanded game."

On December 7, 1941, the Japanese bombed Pearl Harbor, and the United States finally entered the war. Franco sent a congratulatory note to the Japanese emperor. Six months later he raised the "Blue Division" — at least 18,000 Spanish volunteers to fight with Nazi divisions against the Soviets on the eastern front.

When World War II began to shift in favor of the Allies, Franco shifted allegiances. In 1944 he called home what was left of the Blue Division and helped the Allies by offering them the use of Spanish ports and air bases and providing Spanish spies. As the Axis began to falter, the pictures of Mussolini and Hitler disappeared from Franco's desk. Now he was interested in courting the United States, wealthy and virtually unscathed by the war.

But it was not simple. It would take Franco six years to get American aid. Franco's enemies placed tremendous pressure on President Franklin D. Roosevelt not to deal with Franco. In an effort to persuade Roosevelt, Franco made a few token moves. In 1945 he announced a general amnesty for political offenders and released a few prisoners. He stopped calling his regime fascist and referred to it as "an organized democracy," setting up a puppet Cortes. In 1947 he declared that Spain was a monarchy and that he was regent. No king would assume the throne while Franco was alive.

German forces occupy Paris. Even with the powerful Nazi war machine on its northern border, Spain maintained an official neutral policy throughout World War II — a delicate balancing act for Franco, who wanted to be certain that Spain would not be on the losing side.

UPI/BETTMANN NEWSPHOTOS

Hitler and Franco review Nazi troops during a meeting at Hendaye on the French-Spanish border. After the vast German aid lent to Franco, Hitler felt betrayed by the Spaniard's insistence on remaining neutral during World War II.

In April 1945, at the San Francisco conference to launch the United Nations, a resolution was passed that barred nations "whose regimes have been established with the aid of armed forces of countries that have fought against the UN, as long as those regimes continue in power." Franco's Spain was the target. In 1946 a UN Security Council resolution unanimously condemned the Franco regime, continuing to bar Spain from UN conferences and affiliated agencies. As the United States started to pour billions of dollars of aid into rebuilding postwar Germany and Japan, Franco received nothing. Despite the cold shoulder, Franco refused to beg. He did not change his politics; the Western nations changed theirs.

A war without bullets, a war of words — a Cold War — spread over the world. Who would control the ruins of Europe — the United States or the Soviet Union? During World War II the Allies had been friends, but now a barrage of anti-Soviet and anti-American propaganda flowed back and forth. Anticommunism became the favorite political pastime in the United States, taking the place of antifascism. Many Americans were accused of being leftist and were blacklisted, hounded, and often fired. Franco's anticommunist and antidemocratic ideas had found a home in the United States.

Ambassadors from the Western democracies started slipping back into Madrid. Economic aid soon followed them. In November 1950 the UN General Assembly passed a resolution revoking earlier UN recommendations on Spain. There was protest around the world, but only silence in the United States, where anyone criticizing Franco's Spain might be called a "red" and lose his or her job.

Patience was something Franco had nurtured. He watched the favorable developments and waited. His daughter, Carmen, married a prominent surgeon in 1950, and he soon had a grandson.

On July 16, 1951, the United States chief of naval operations, Admiral Forrest Sherman, had talks with Generalissimo Franco about the possibility of the United States establishing air and naval bases in Spain. They had one belief in common — anticommunism. Franco had one huge advantage — the United States needed Spain. Now he could bargain in earnest from a position of power.

Franco's neutral policies turn a profit as a U.S. relief ship heads for Spain during the 1940s. As soon as it became evident that the Allies were winning the war, Franco offered them the use of Spanish ports, hoping to reap the postwar benefits of friendship.

AMERICAN RELIEF
+
SHIP FOR SPAIN

A Spanish farmer surveys his prospering land during the 1950s. In 1953 Spain became a U.S. ally and with extensive Western aid began its recovery from a long era of economic instability.

AP/WIDE WORLD PHOTOS

In 1953 a pact was signed, and Franco's Spain became the ally of the most powerful country in the world. (Almost as a result of this pact, Spain was asked to join the United Nations in 1955.) U.S. air bases in Spain would put American bombers within 3,000 miles of the industrial centers of the Soviet Union. American naval bases on Spain's coasts helped to make the United States a postwar naval power in the Mediterranean. In exchange, Franco got millions of dollars in U.S. economic aid.

In 1957 alone, credits and aid from the United States to Franco's Spain totaled over $350 million. Another $100 million of agricultural surplus was sent. The United States had refused to save the republic, but it was making vast contributions to the stability of a fascist Spain under Franco.

Using his U.S. connections, Franco attracted foreign investment and developed inexpensive tourism. He offered tax concessions, cheap labor, and high profits. A new middle class developed. The poor did not benefit much, but many of them were able to migrate and take on menial jobs in the booming economies of nearby European states.

Franco thanked President Dwight D. Eisenhower in person in 1959. On a tour, Eisenhower was invited by the Spanish ambassador to make a stop in Spain, where no U.S. president had ever set foot. By then there was a $400-million chain of American bases in Spain, and it was unwise for the United States government to be discourteous, so Eisenhower accepted.

Met by Franco in person when he landed, Eisenhower was at first cold and formal. But Franco had the streets of Madrid ready. Thousands cheered from the sidewalks as television cameras recorded the event. On a floodlit balcony, Señora Carmen, her daughter and son-in-law, and four little grandchildren were smiling. Eisenhower courteously lifted his hat to them and thousands cheered.

That evening a glorious banquet was laid out for the visitor. Franco thanked the American nation for its aid, stating, "We . . . owe the peace we enjoy and the preservation of Western Europe against falling under the Communist yoke to your energy and gen-

Franco and his grandson Francisco hunt on the family estate of El Pardo, a few miles north of Madrid. During the 1960s Franco spent an increasing amount of time at home with his family.

erosity." Now there were just two anticommunists, Franco and Eisenhower, breaking bread together. The band played "Yellow Rose of Texas" and "The Star-Spangled Banner."

The next morning the two leaders ate breakfast together, joking and chatting amiably. As Eisenhower prepared to leave, television newsreel cameramen surrounded them. Eisenhower was no longer cold to the Spanish dictator. He threw his arms around Franco in the typical Spanish *abrazo*, a big hug, and Franco hugged him back.

That year, as usual, the veterans of the Abraham Lincoln Battalion had their reunion. Fewer of them were alive and all were showing their age. The man who had murdered the Spanish Republic was now a respected member of the world community and they, the veterans of the Abraham Lincoln Battalion, were blacklisted, despised, and hunted. The most courageous defenders of democracy were considered traitors.

After Franco's successful revolution in 1939 an ominous repression ruled Spain. Visitors commented on the eerie silence — workers at bars were

A woman hangs out her wash on a hilltop overlooking the bleak vista of Barcelona. The poor in Franco's Spain, who suffered under a severe tax burden, did not enjoy the economic benefits brought about by Western aid to the country.

not talking about anything except the weather, health, and family. A fearful peace prevailed. From father to son the bloody story of the civil war was passed on and with it the warning to avoid another. Spain remained a land of terrible contradictions. Lavish tourist hotels dotted the Mediterranean within view of absolute squalor.

Elsewhere in the world, changes were taking place. In the United States the Cold War drew to an end as more and more people recognized the importance of peaceful coexistence in a nuclear world. In the 1960s popular movements for civil rights for blacks and equality for women swept over the United States. In Europe, too, youth demanded more freedom and better living conditions. Dictators, many of them friends of Franco — Fulgencio Batista in Cuba, Antonio de Oliveira Salazar in Portugal — were swept out of power, and colonies fought for and won their independence.

In 1959, Spain became an associate member of the Organization for European Economic Cooperation and began to receive assistance from the International Monetary Fund. American banks offered $418 million in loans for an economic stabilization program. Spain's request for membership in the European Economic Community (EEC), however, was tabled until Franco's government agreed to carry out democratic reforms. Spain would not be admitted to the EEC while Franco was alive. The Spanish economy improved, but political tensions were growing beneath the surface. By the early 1960s there emerged diverse political factions in Spain, and the country began to experience widespread labor unrest. Protests by workers, such as the 1962 Asturias miners' strike in the northwest, compelled Franco to make concessions. He made several cabinet changes and, in 1964, pardoned a number of civil-war political prisoners. Two years later he ratified a new constitution, which granted greater political and religious freedoms and provided a nominal separation of power between the chief of state and the head of government, the country's two highest officials. Still, political unrest, particularly among students, persisted, and in 1969 Franco responded by severely censoring the press and declaring a two-month state of emergency, during which personal freedoms were strictly limited.

Franco (center) enjoys a visit by his appointed successor, Prince Juan Carlos (left), and Paraguayan leader, General Alfredo Stroessner. Juan Carlos, the grandson of Alphonso XIII, was not given any real authority until the death of Franco.

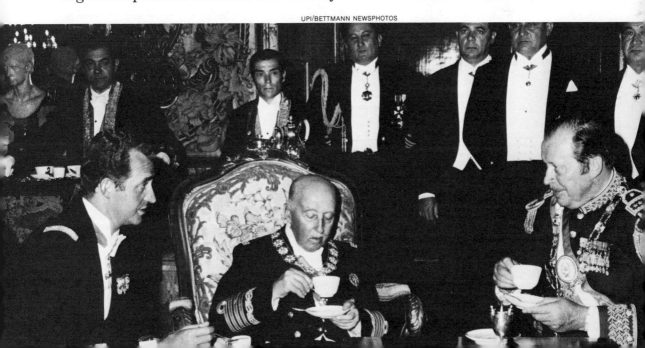

Though his active role during the tumultuous 1960s as head of state might suggest otherwise, Franco was mellowing. Less fearful of opposition, he began to spend more time at home, playing with his seven grandchildren and enjoying his gardens. He went to church more and more frequently, perhaps thinking about his own death.

In 1942 Franco had ordered the construction of a huge mausoleum known as the Valley of the Fallen. It was dedicated on April 1, 1959. Carved into a mountainside, its 500-foot-high cross can be seen 30 miles away in Madrid. Mention of the cost of this immense structure was forbidden, but much of the labor was carried out by political prisoners. Franco claimed it was built in memory of the dead on both sides of the civil war, but in Spain it was commonly regarded as Franco's personal monument and tomb.

In 1969, aging and ill, Franco designated Prince Juan Carlos de Bourbón, grandson of King Alfonso XIII, who had lost his throne in 1931, as his successor. However, even during his last years, when he suffered heart attack after heart attack, Franco refused to transfer power. On November 20, 1975, he finally died.

Except for the United States, which had Vice-President Nelson Rockefeller attend, none of the Western democracies sent high-ranking officials to Franco's funeral or to the inauguration ceremonies for King

The unfinished crypt of General Francisco Franco at the Valley of the Fallen near Madrid. Three years after the fascist's death, in response to popular pressure Spain once again became a democratic republic.

Franco's wife, Carmen, and daughter mourn the loss of their illustrious husband and father. The Spanish generalissimo passed away on November 20, 1975, after a series of severe heart attacks.

Juan Carlos I. Richard Nixon, former president of the United States, commented that Franco had earned respect for Spain through "firmness and fairness."

Franco was buried in the vast crypt at the Valley of the Fallen. As king, Juan Carlos initially attempted to rule under Franco's authoritarian principles, but pressures for freedom quickly mounted. Faced with protests and demonstrations, in 1977 the king was forced to allow the first free elections in 41 years. On December 29, 1978, Spain became once again a constitutional republic, with an elected Cortes passing laws. The king held only a ceremonial role. Catalonia and the Basque country were given regional autonomy. Over a thousand political prisoners who had managed to outlive Franco were pardoned. Controls on the press were loosened, and the communist and socialist parties, previously outlawed, became legal once again.

High on the mountaintop, Franco's giant cross is illuminated every night, a sorrowful reminder of bloody civil war and of the tyrant who ruled Spain for 36 years.

Further Reading

Brome, Vincent. *The International Brigades.* New York: William Morrow and Co., 1966.

Coles, S. F. A. *Franco of Spain.* Westminster, MD: Newman Press, 1956.

Crozier, Brian. *Franco.* Boston: Little Brown and Co., 1967.

Feis, Herbert. *The Spanish Story: Franco and the Nations at War.* New York: Alfred A. Knopf, 1948.

Goldston, Robert. *The Civil War in Spain.* New York: Bobbs-Merrill Co., 1966.

Jackson, Gabriel. *A Concise History of the Spanish Civil War.* New York: The John Day Co., 1974.

Landis, Arthur H. *The Abraham Lincoln Brigade.* New York: Citadel Press, 1967.

Lloyd, Alan. *Franco.* Garden City, NY: Doubleday & Co., Inc., 1969.

Matthews, Herbert L. *The Yoke and the Arrows.* New York: George Braziller, Inc., 1957.

Payne, Robert, ed. *The Civil War in Spain, 1936–39.* New York: G.P. Putnam's Sons, 1962.

Thomas, Hugh. *The Spanish Civil War.* New York: Harper & Brothers, Publishers, 1961.

Trythall, J. W. D. *El Caudillo — A Political Biography of Franco.* New York: McGraw-Hill Book Co., 1970.

Yglesias, José. *The Franco Years.* New York: Bobbs-Merrill Co., Inc., 1977.

Chronology

Dec. 4, 1892	Born Francisco Paulino Hermenegildo Teódulo Franco y Bahamonde in El Ferrol, Spain
1907–10	Studies at the Infantry Academy at Toledo
1912	Assigned to the Morocco garrison
Oct. 1920	Serves as second in command of the Spanish Foreign Legion
June 1923	Appointed head of the Spanish Foreign Legion
Sept. 13, 1923	Primo de Rivera becomes dictator of Spain after military coup d'état
Oct. 22, 1923	Franco marries Carmen Polo y Martínez Valdés
1925	Successful joint French and Spanish invasion of Morocco and defeat of rebel leader Abd el-Krim
	Franco is promoted to brigadier general
	Becomes head of new military academy at Zaragoza
1930	Primo de Rivera resigns as dictator
April 1931	Republicans triumph in municipal elections; King Alfonso XIII leaves Spain
July 1931	Franco's military academy is closed
Feb. 1932	Given command of an infantry brigade in La Corunna
March 1933	Sent to command the military in the Balearic Islands
Oct. 1934	Crushes a miners' strike in Asturias
Feb. 1935	Named commander in chief of armed forces in Morocco
May 1935	Recalled to Madrid to become chief of the army's central staff
Feb. 1936	Election victory of the republican Popular Front party
1936	Franco joins a conspiracy to overthrow the republic, opening the Spanish Civil War
Oct. 1, 1936	Declares himself supreme commander of the armed forces and chief of state
April 26, 1937	Germans bomb Guernica
April 1, 1939	Nationalists win the war; Franco becomes dictator of all Spain
Sept. 1939	World War II begins
Oct. 23, 1940	Franco meets with Adolf Hitler at Hendaye
April 1945	United Nations bars Spain from membership
1953	United States signs pact with Franco to build military bases in Spain
1955	Spain is asked to join the United Nations
1959	U.S. President Eisenhower visits Spain
1969	Franco designates Prince Juan Carlos de Bourbòn as his successor
Nov. 20, 1975	Dies in Madrid

Index

George V, king of Great Britain, 62
George Washington Battalion, 16
Germany, 13, 14, 16, 27, 35, 54, 70–71, 80, 82, 88–89, 94–95, 98, 100
Gil Robles, José Maria, 53, 55–56, 59, 61
Goering, Hermann, 70, 82
Great Britain, 13, 20, 27, 62, 71, 89, 93, 95
Great Depression, the, 44
Guadalajara, 69, 82
Guam, 20, 21, 24
Guernica, 82, 84
Hadda-Allal-u-Kaddar, 32
Hidalgo, Diego, 56–57
Hitler, Adolf, 13, 53, 70–71, 82, 88–89, 96–99
Ibarruri, Dolores, 68
Iberian Anarchist Federation (FAI), 46
International Monetary Fund, 105
Italy, 13–14, 16, 46, 54, 82, 85, 89–90, 94
Japan, 94, 98, 100
Juan Carlos I (Juan Carlos de Bourbon), king of Spain, 106–107
La Corunna, 51
La Pasionaria, 19, 68, 74
Largo Caballero, Francisco, 54, 59, 77, 80, 85, 93
Law of Political Responsibilities, 90
Le Havre, 14
Lerroux, Alejandro, 53, 55–56, 59
London, 62
Lorca, Federico García, 74
Loyalist Militia, 69
Madrid, 17, 48, 51–53, 55–56, 58, 65, 67, 68, 72–73, 74, 77, 80, 90–91, 93, 101
Maceo, Antonio, 23
Maine, U.S.S., 23
Majorca, 88
Martí, José, 23
Melilla, 31, 36, 38
Merriman, Robert Hale, 81
Mexico, 20, 93
Miaja Menant, José, 80
Millán Astray, José, 35, 37, 71
Mola Vidal, Emilio, 63, 69, 79–80, 82, 86
monarchists, 27, 46, 48, 53, 61, 79
Moroccan Regulares, 57
Morocco, 21, 24, 27, 29, 31–41, 43–44, 59, 67, 69

Moscardó, José, 77
Munich Pact, 89
Mussolini, Benito, 13, 70–71, 96–97, 98–99
National Confederation of Labor (CNT), 49, 85
National Front party, 61, 65
Nationalists, 13, 67–69, 71–72, 74, 80–82, 85, 88, 90
Nazis, 13, 88, 93, 98
Negrín, Juan, 85–87, 90
Nonintervention Committee, 89
Organization for European Economic Cooperation (OEEC), 105
Oviedo, 34, 36–38, 55, 57
Paris, Treaty of, 24
Pearl Harbor, 98
Philippines, 20–21, 24–25
Pius XI, 86
Popular Front, 61–62, 64–65
Portugal, 44, 74, 89–90
Primo de Rivera, José Antonio, 53, 63
Primo de Rivera, Miguel, 38–41, 43–44
Prince's Regiment, 34, 37
Puerto Rico, 21, 24–25
Pyrenees, 16
Queipo de Llano, Gonzalo, 67, 71–72
"red miners," 55–57
Regulares Indígenas (Regular Native Forces), 32
Republicans, 44, 46, 48, 50, 53, 58, 61–62, 71, 80, 82, 85–91, 93
Rockefeller, Nelson, 106
Roman Catholic church, 25, 44, 46, 51, 53, 61
   see also Vatican, the
Roosevelt, Franklin D., 99
Salamanca, 79
Salazar, Antonio de Oliviera, 104
Sanjurjo, José, 44, 47, 51–52, 54, 63, 67, 69
Seville, 47, 51, 67, 71–72
Sherman, Forrest, 101
Silvestre, Manual Fernández, 35
Sirval, Luis, 57
socialism, 29, 44, 48, 51–52, 54, 57, 61, 74, 85, 89
Sotelo, José Calvo, 65
Spanish-American War, 23–25
Spanish Civil War, 13–19, 46–59, 61–65, 67–74, 77–91, 94

Hedda Garza lives in upstate New York, where she works as a freelance writer, editor, and lecturer. Her articles have appeared in several national magazines and her *Watergate Investigation Index* won the best academic book award from *Choice* magazine. She is also the author of *Trotsky* in the Chelsea House series WORLD LEADERS — PAST & PRESENT.

Arthur M. Schlesinger, jr., taught history at Harvard for many years and is currently Albert Schweitzer Professor of the Humanities at City University of New York. He is the author of numerous highly praised works in American history and has twice been awarded the Pulitzer Prize. He served in the White House as special assistant to Presidents Kennedy and Johnson.